HALLOWEEN COLORING BOOK

This Book Belongs to :

____

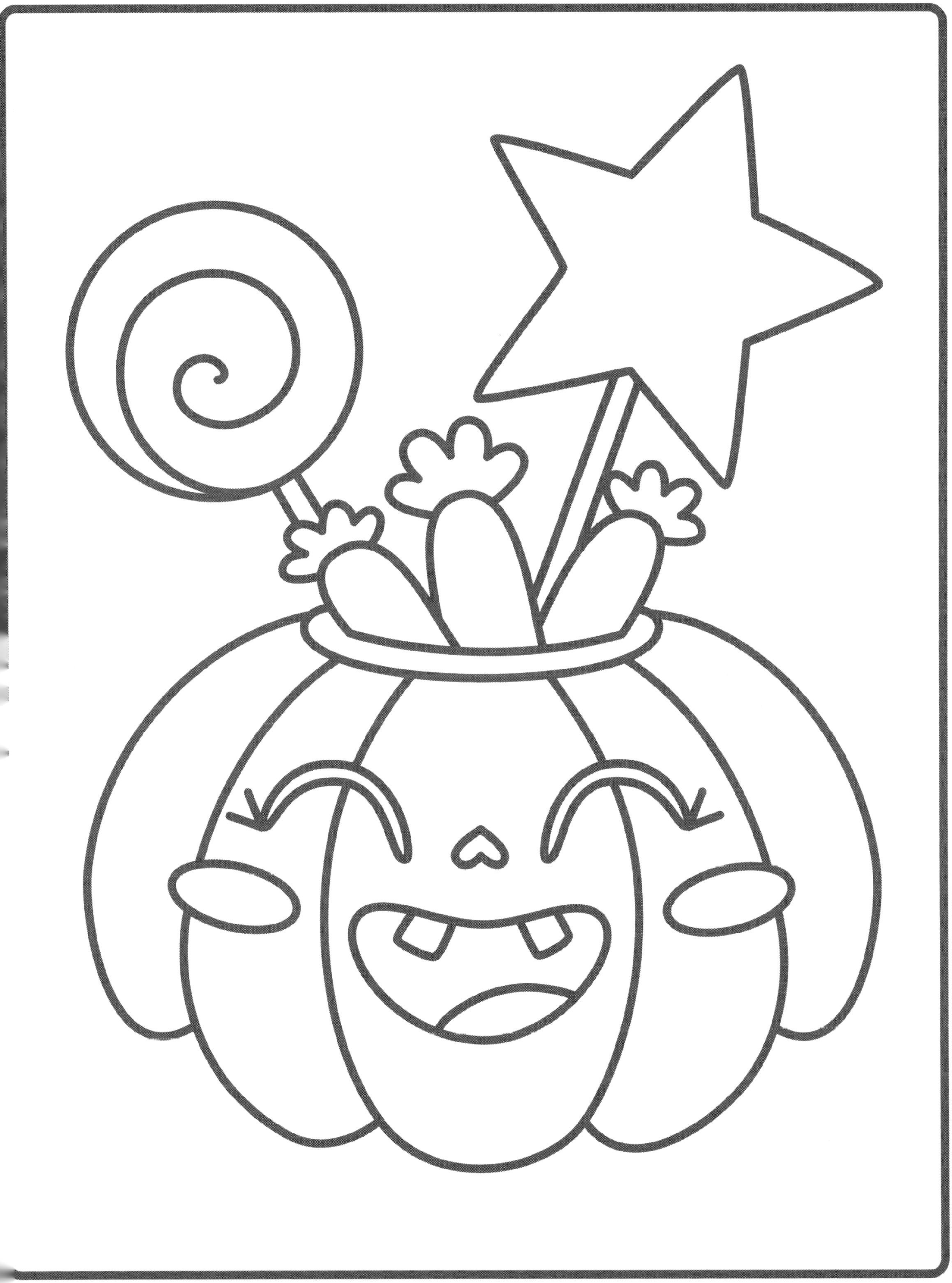

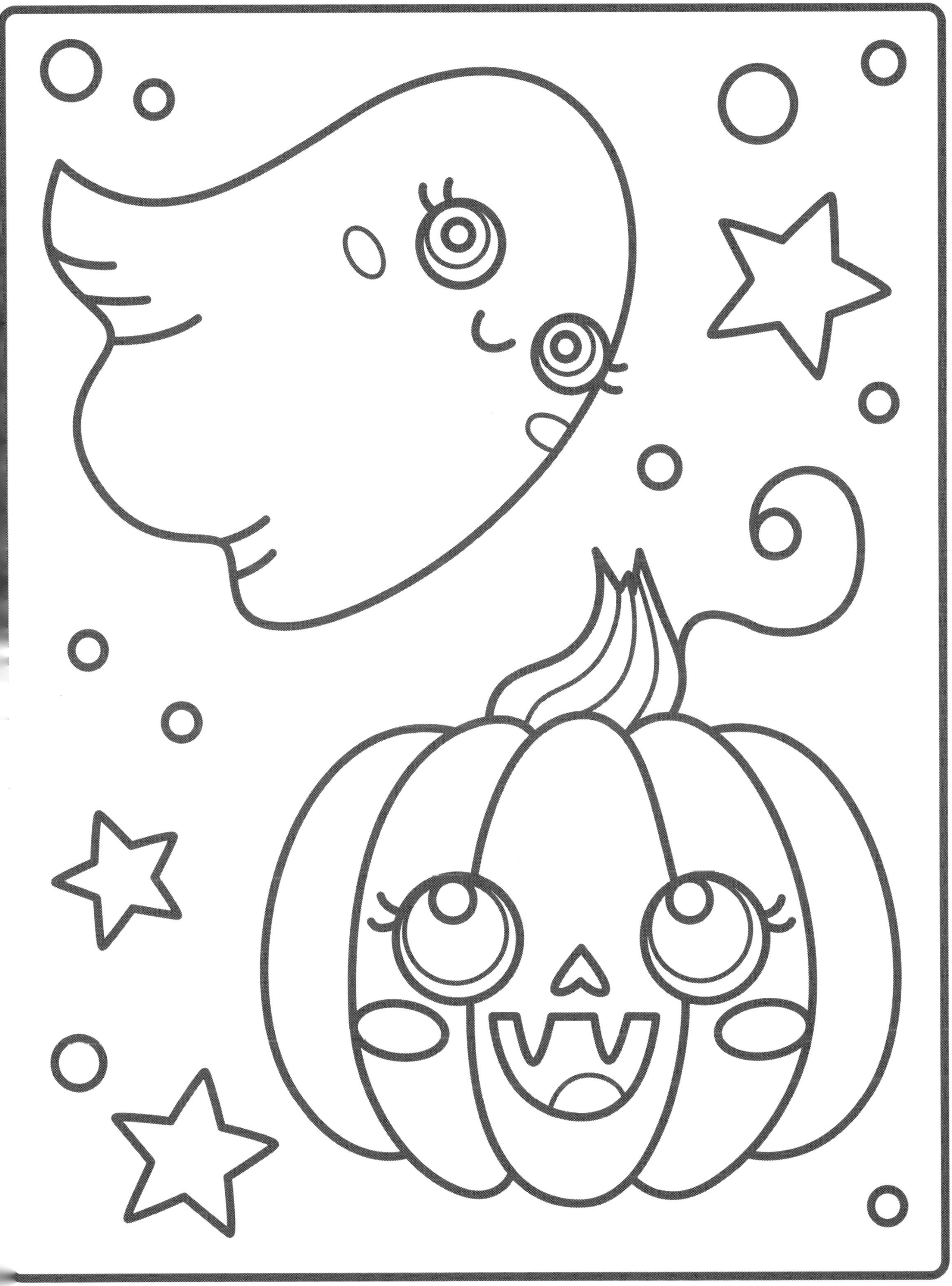

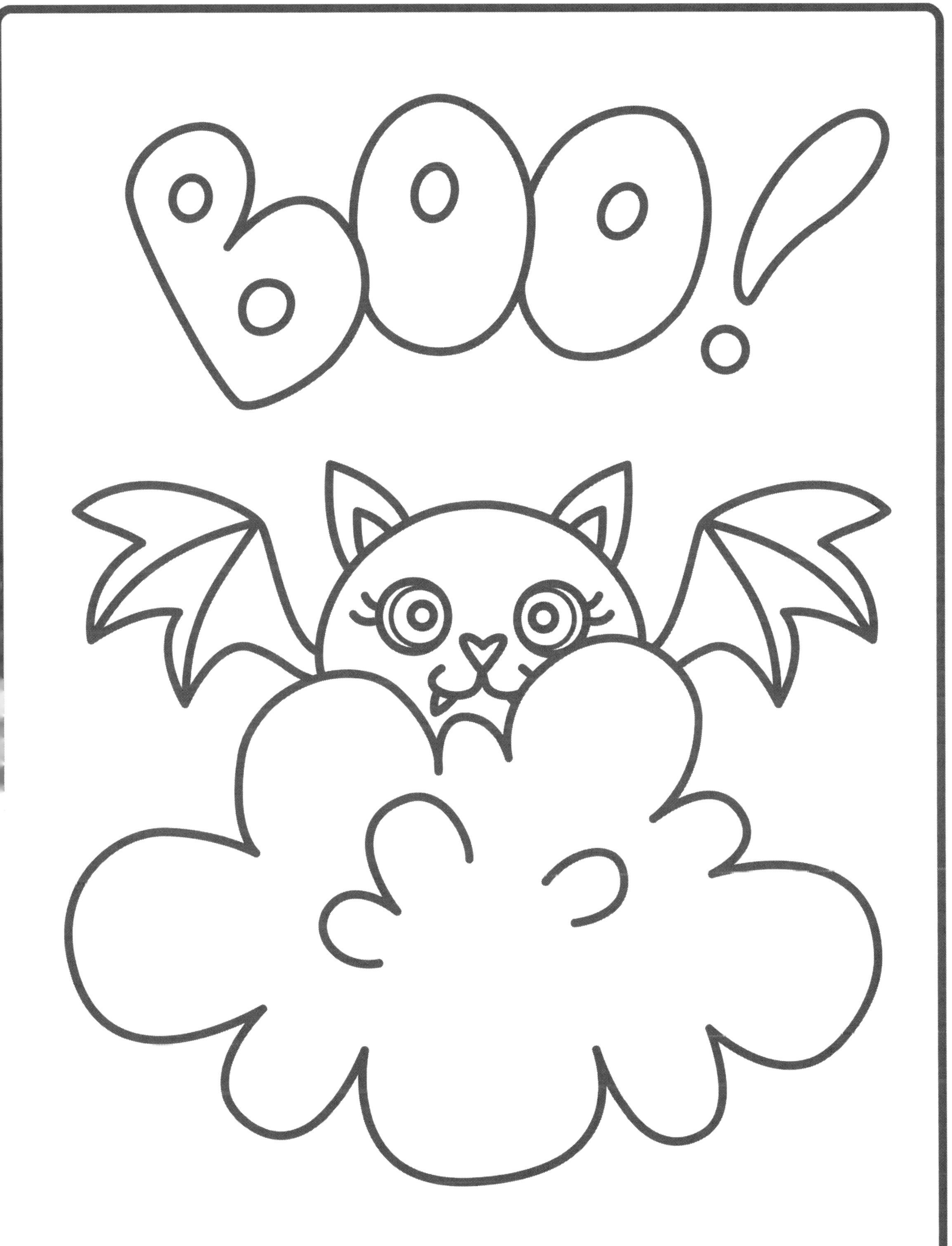
BOO!

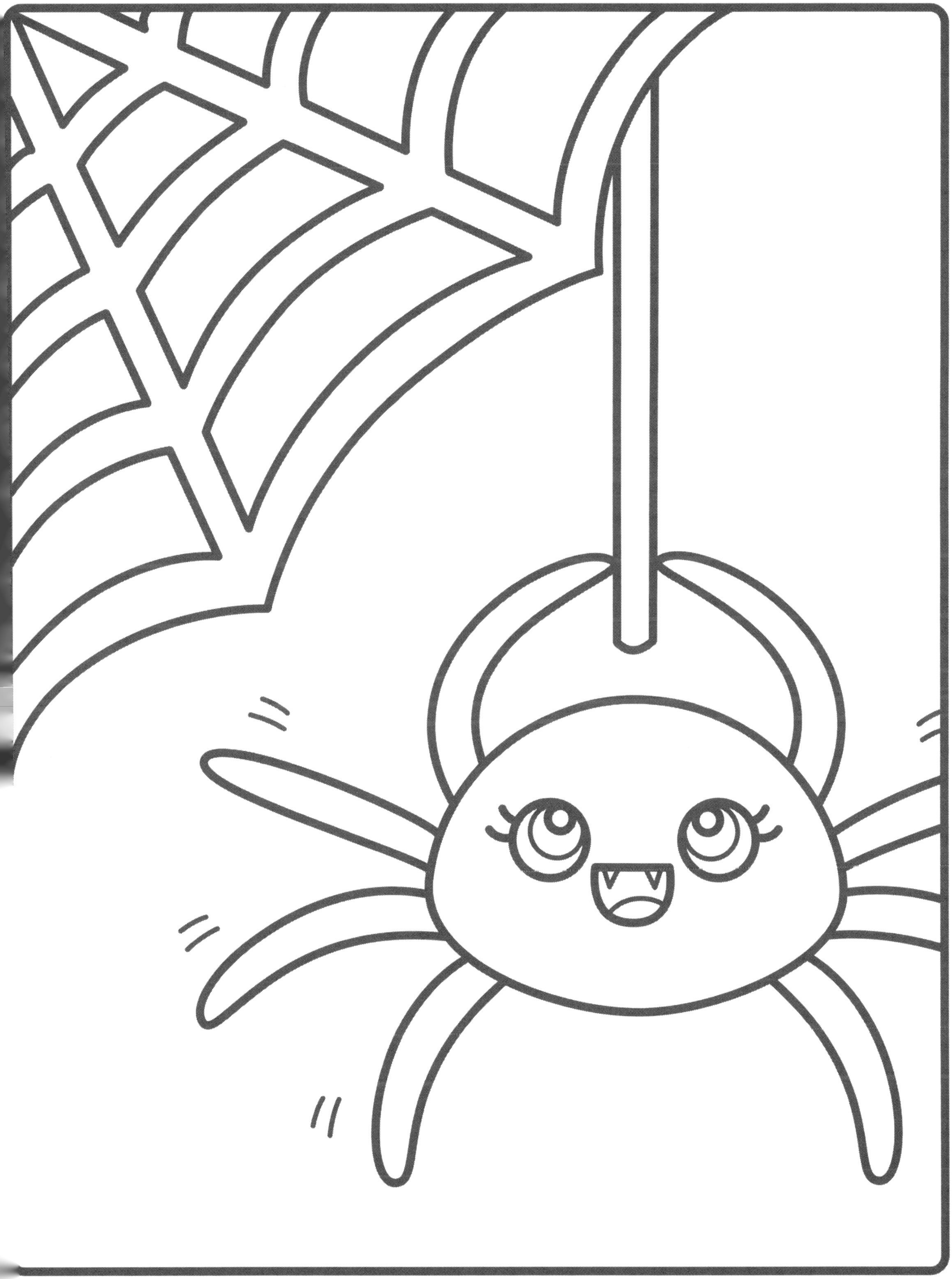

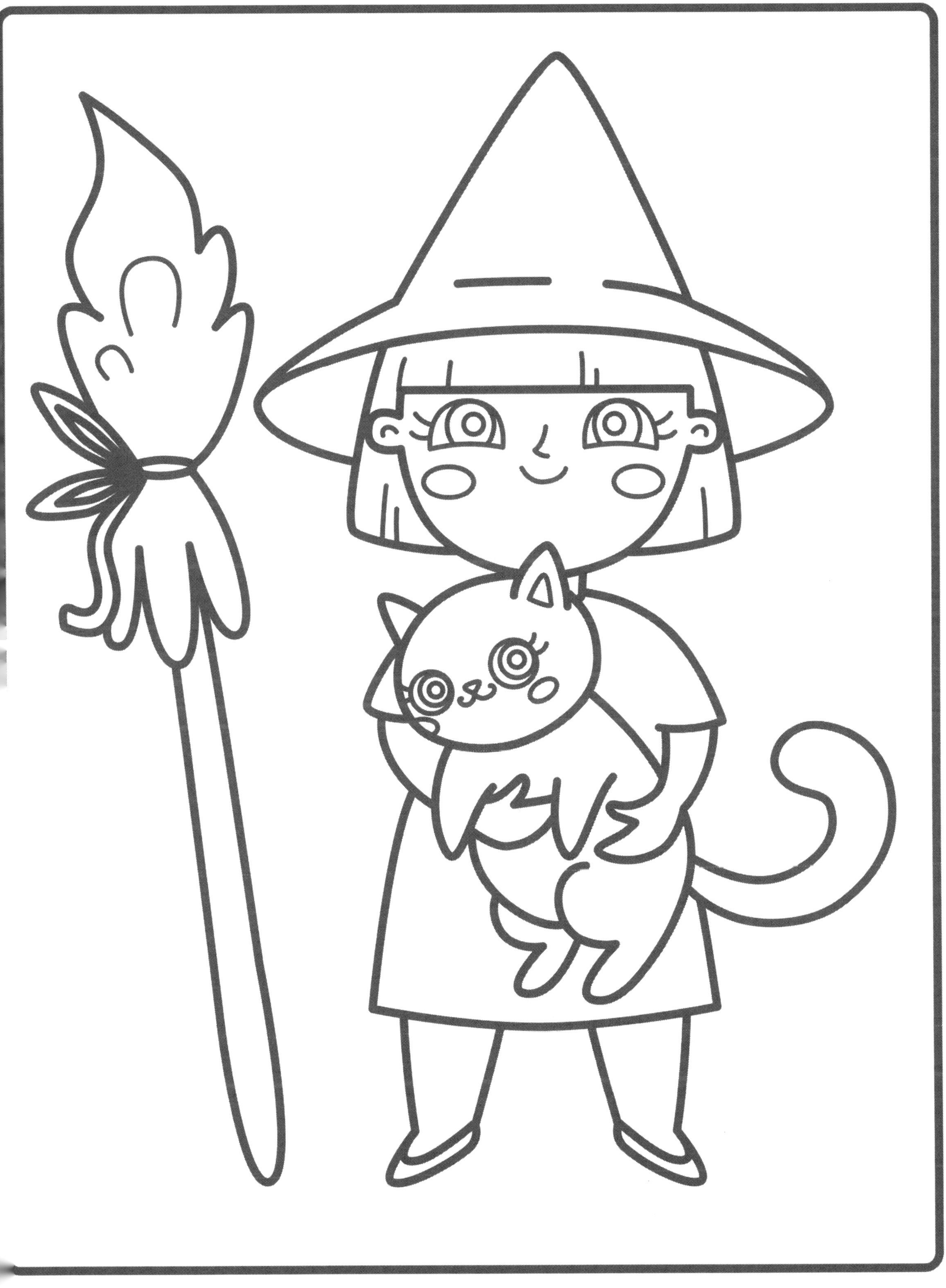

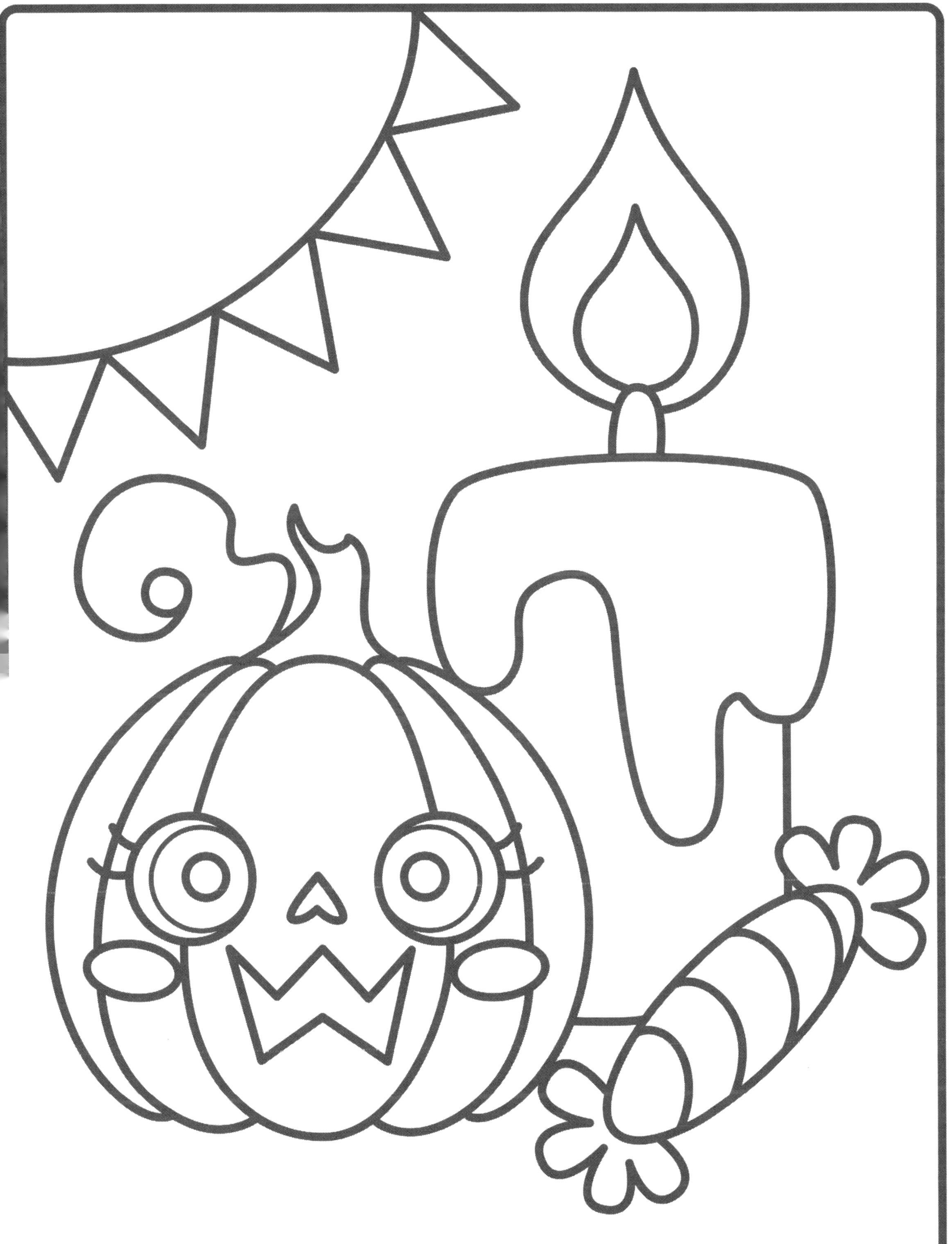

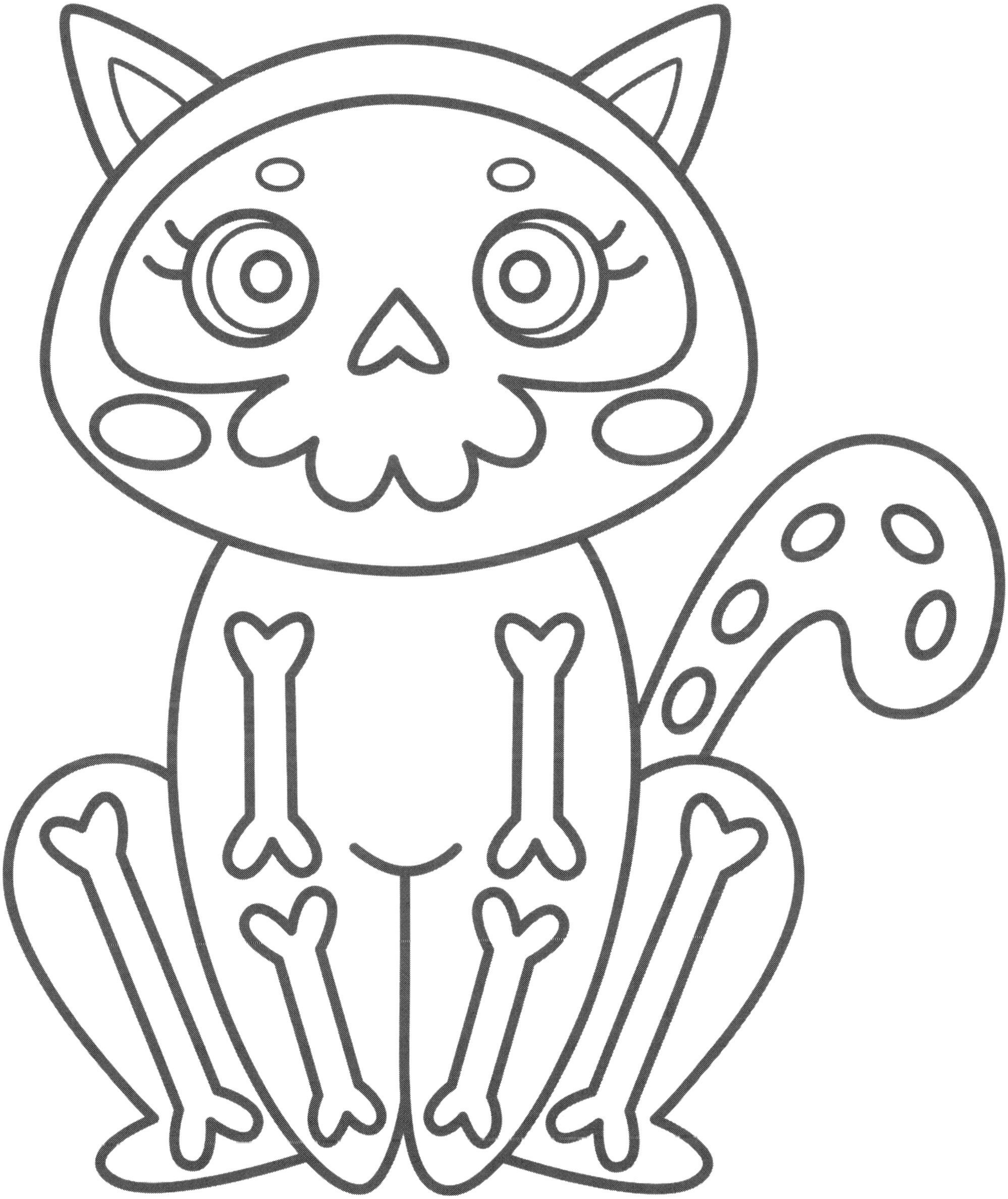

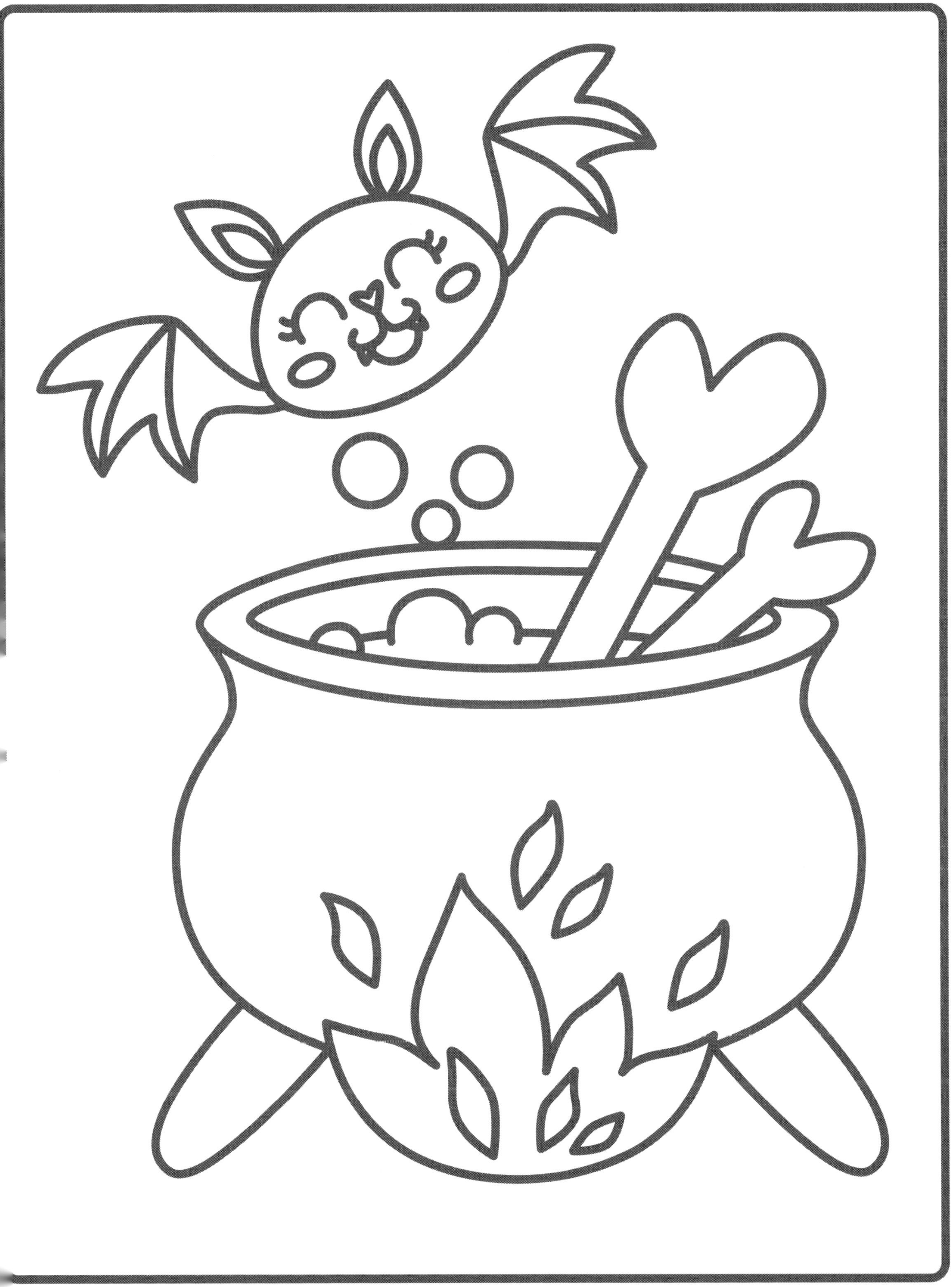

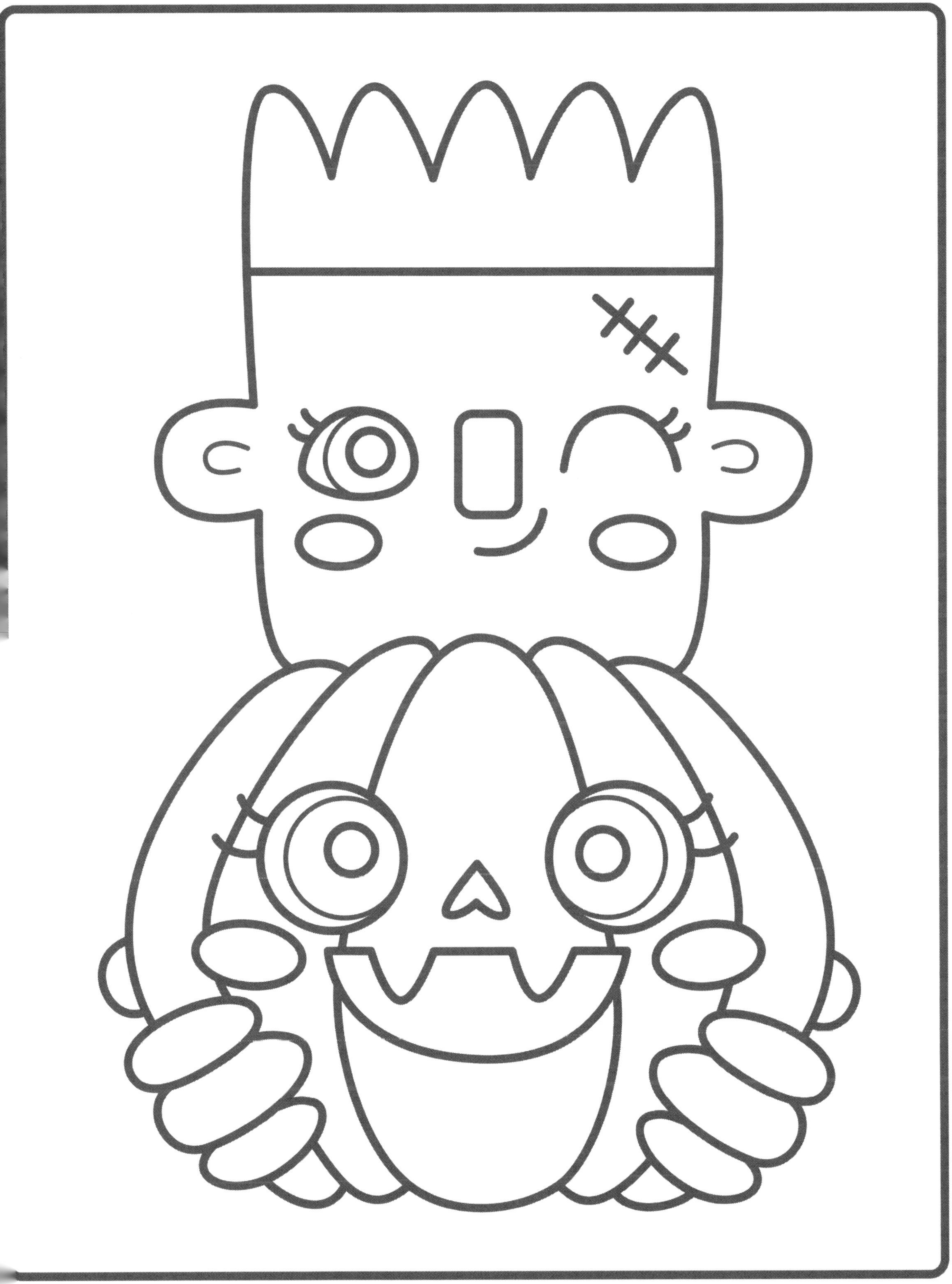

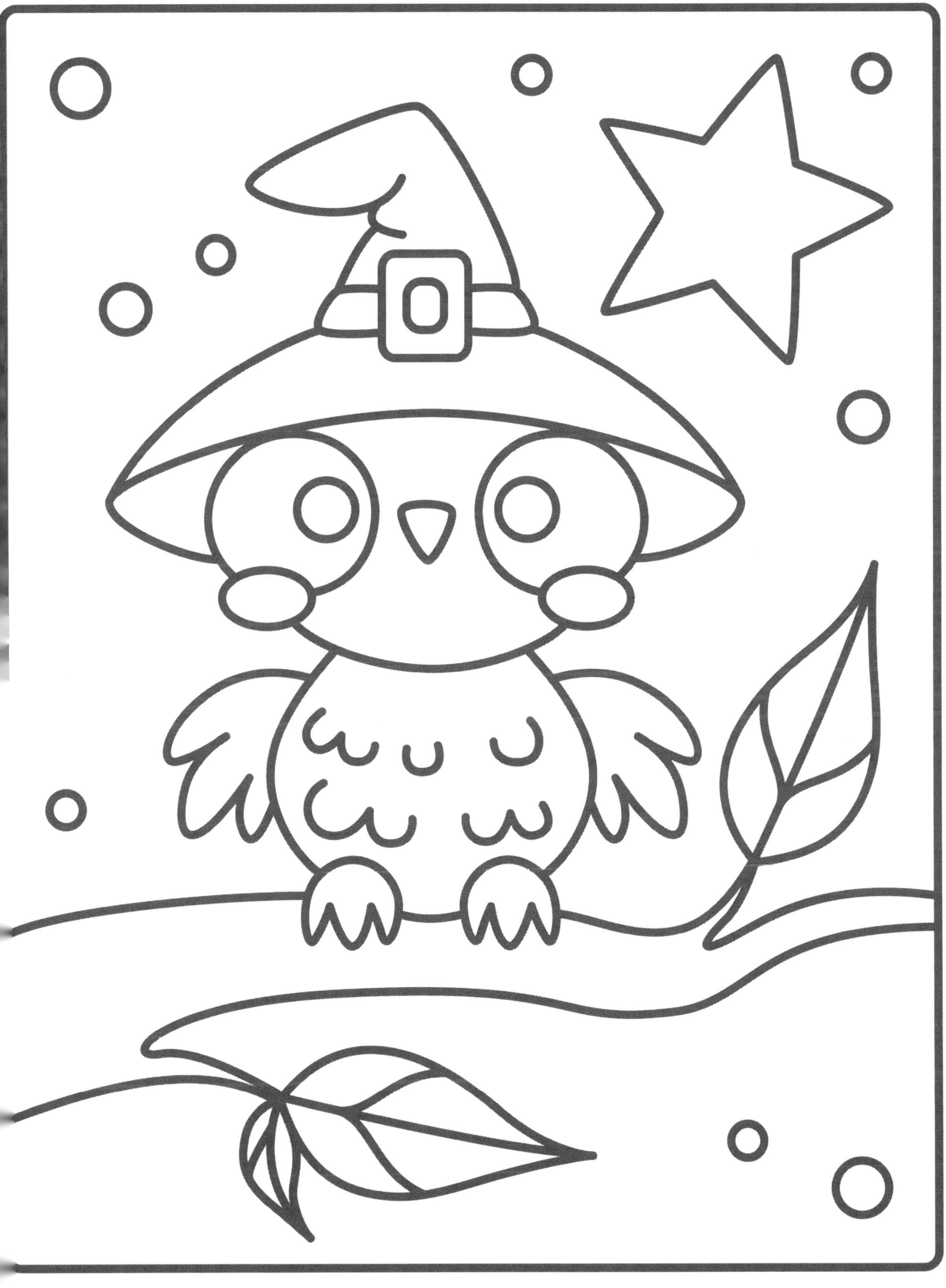

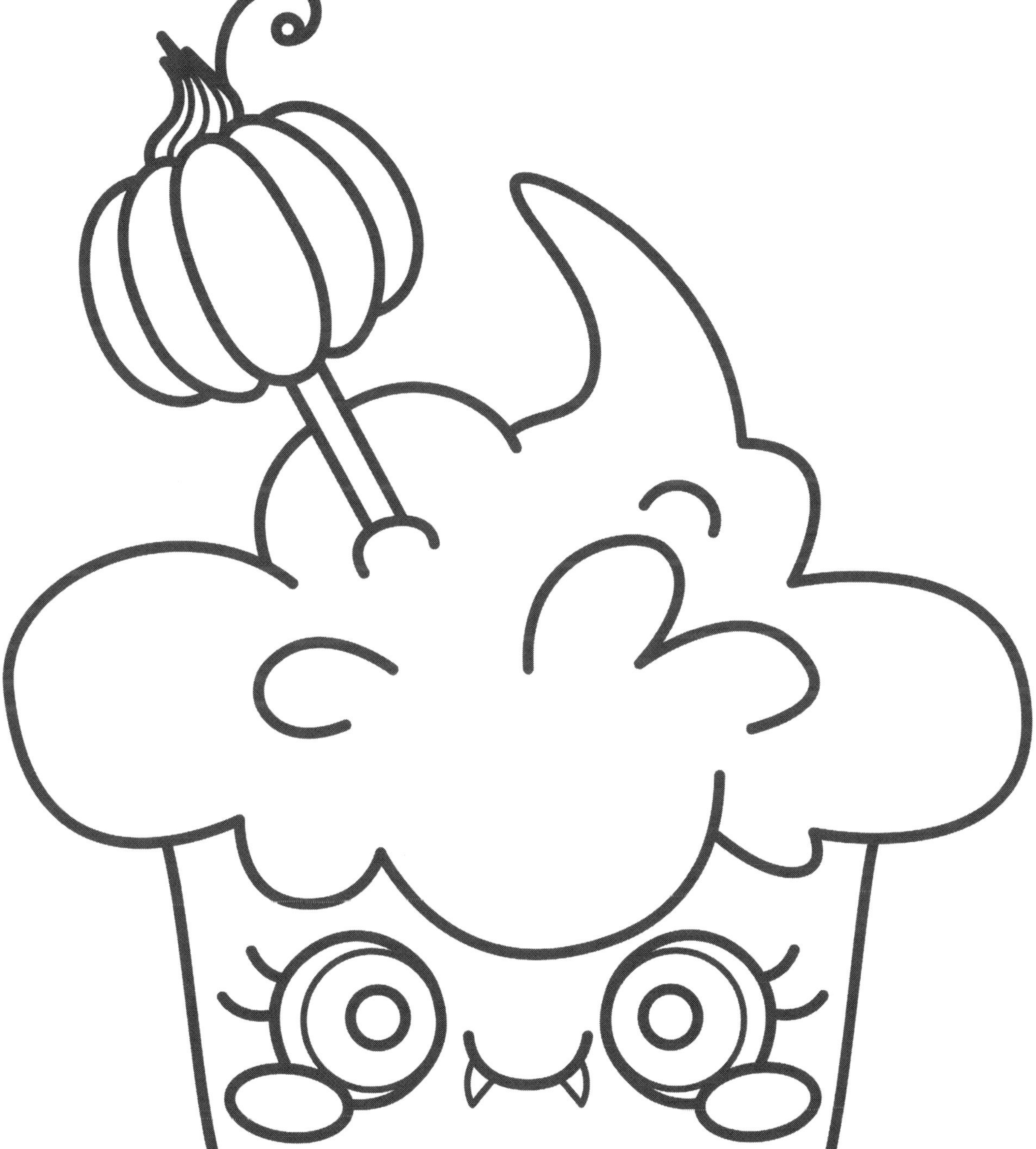

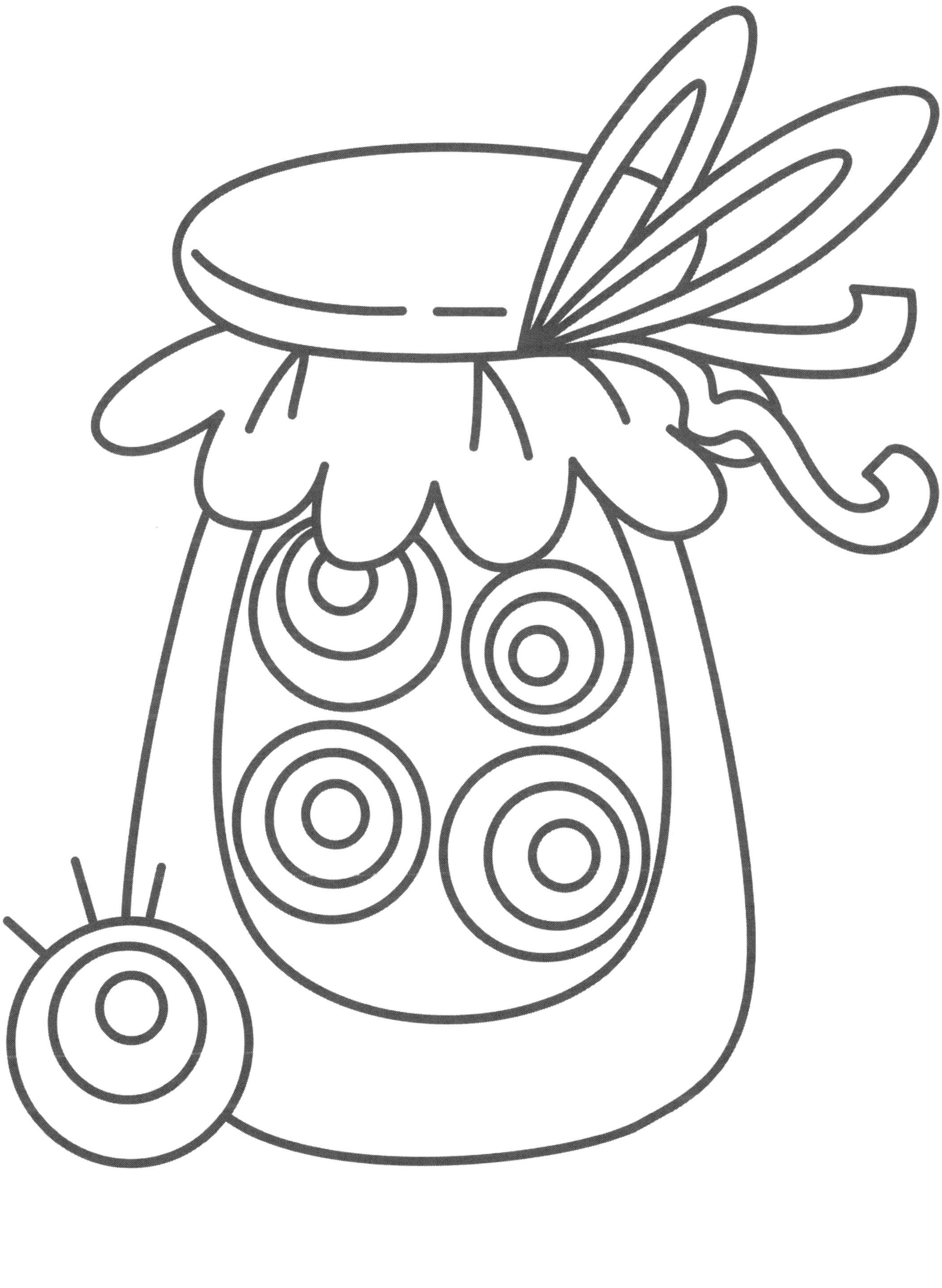

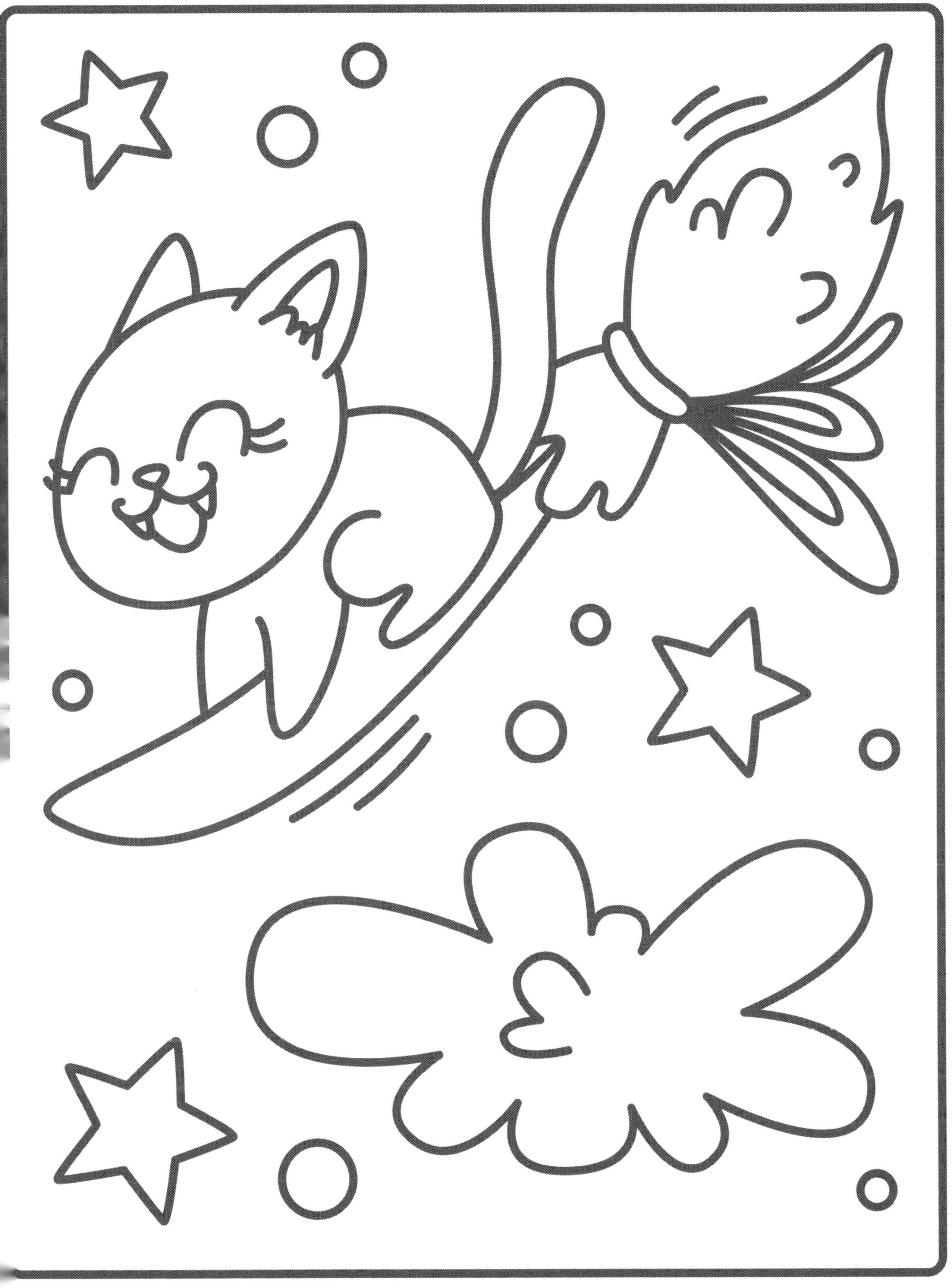

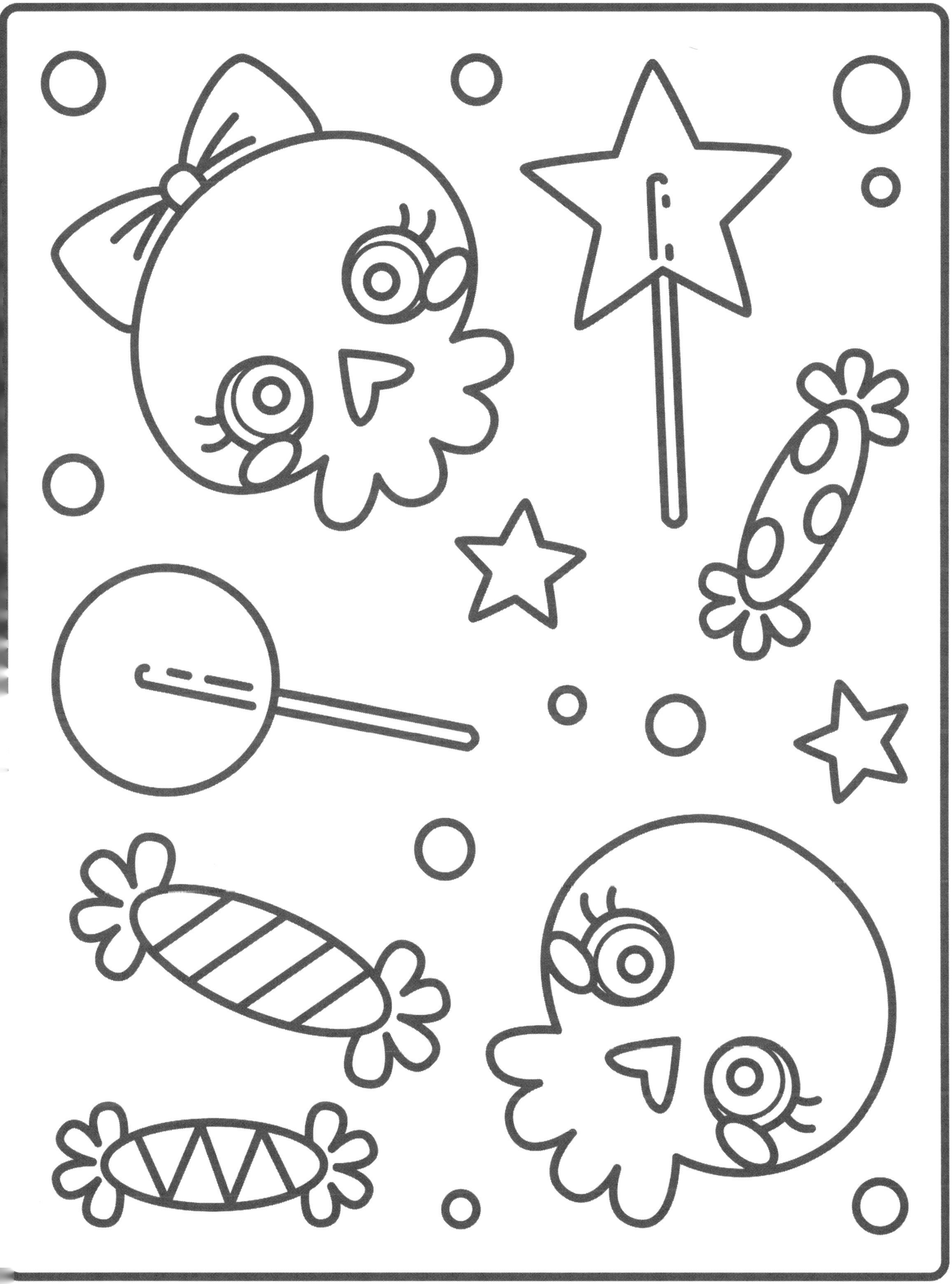

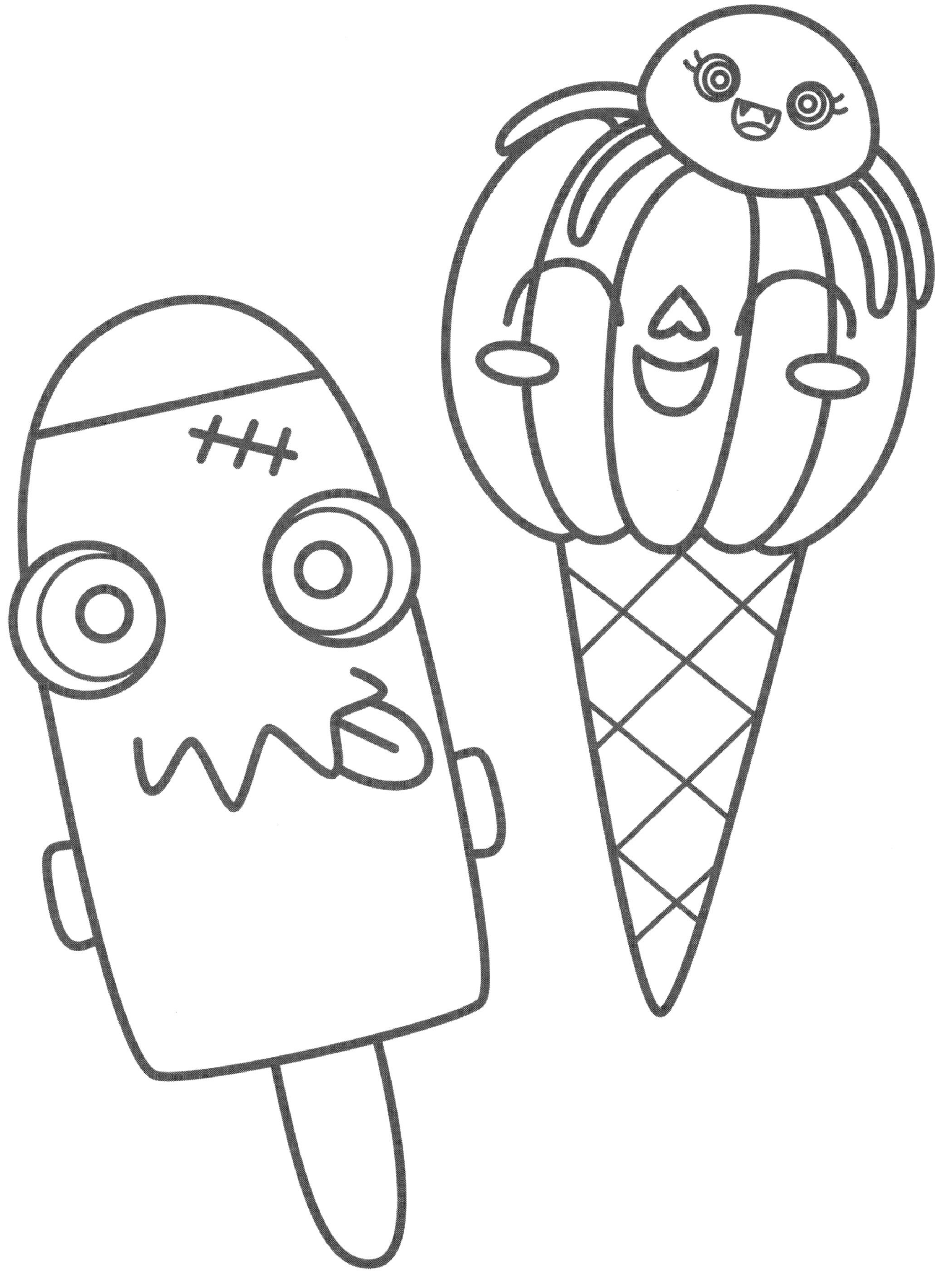

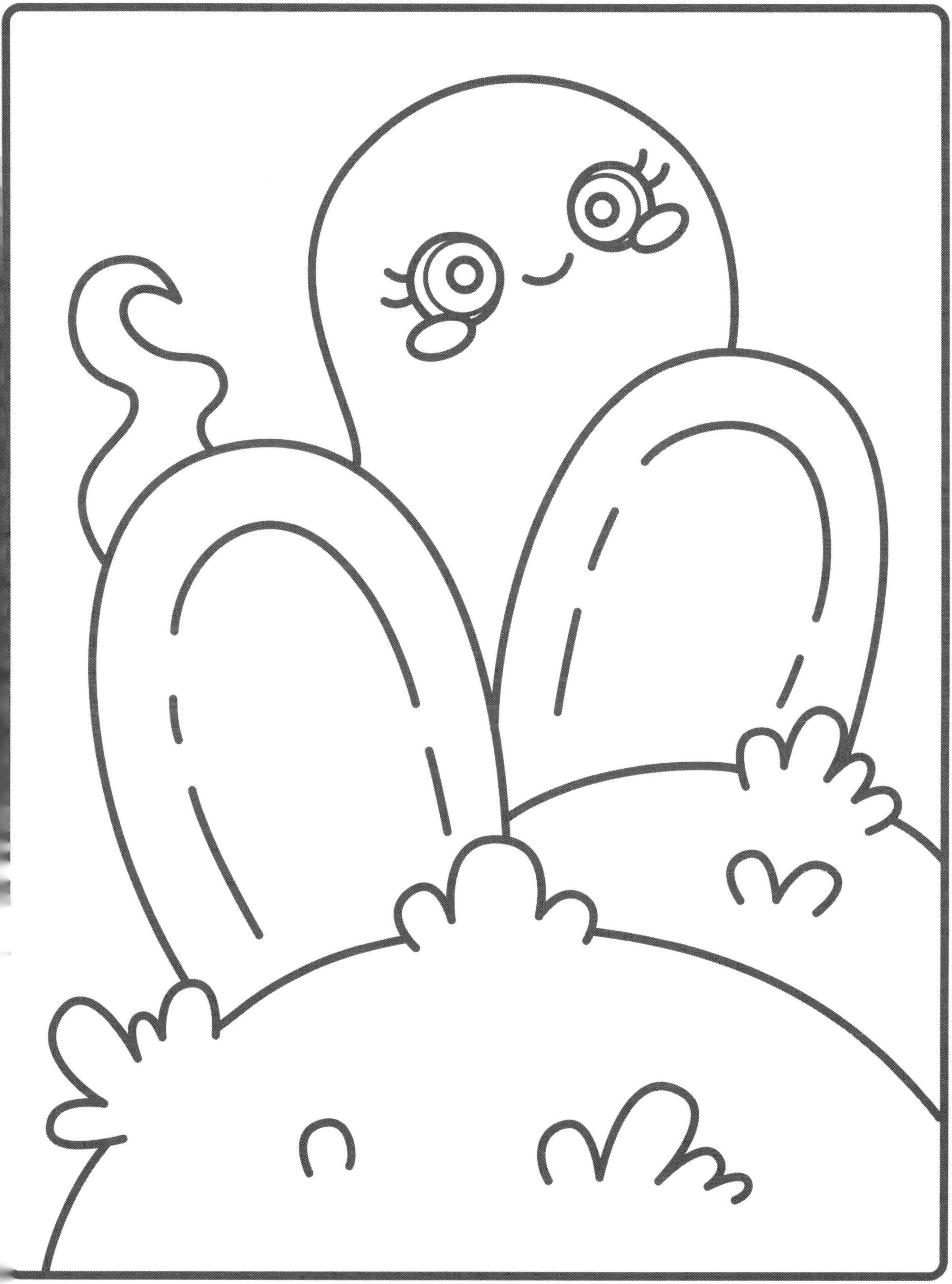

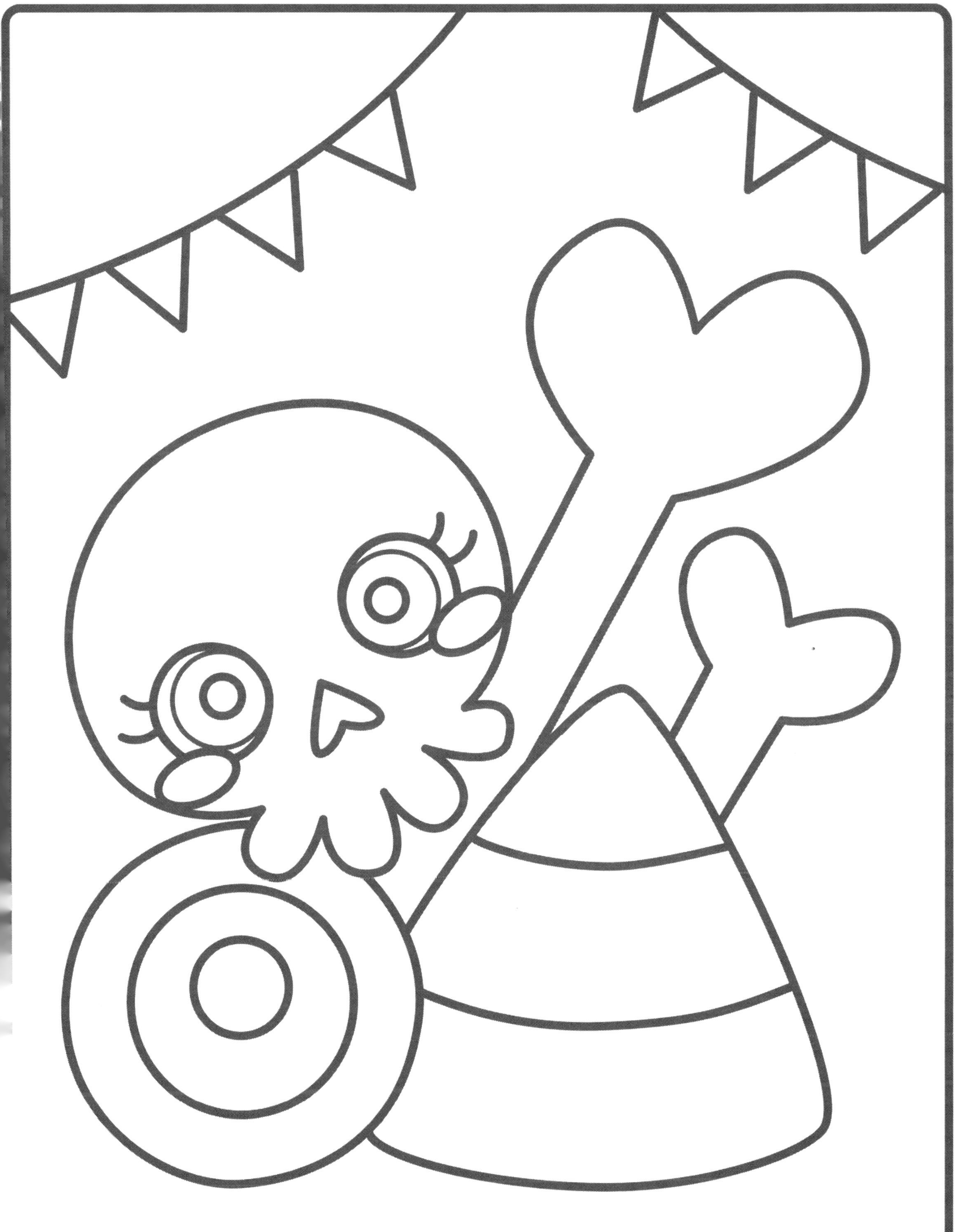

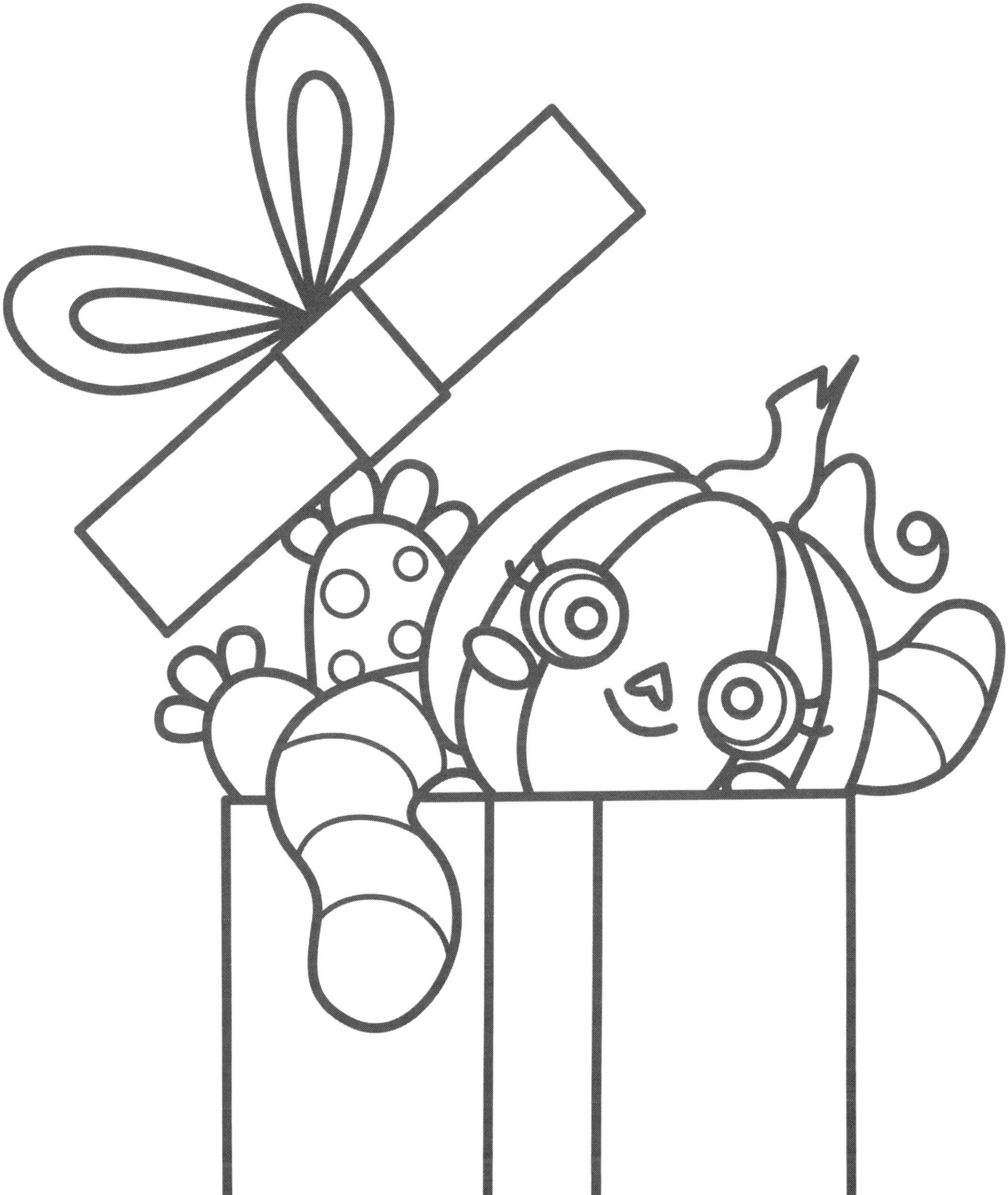

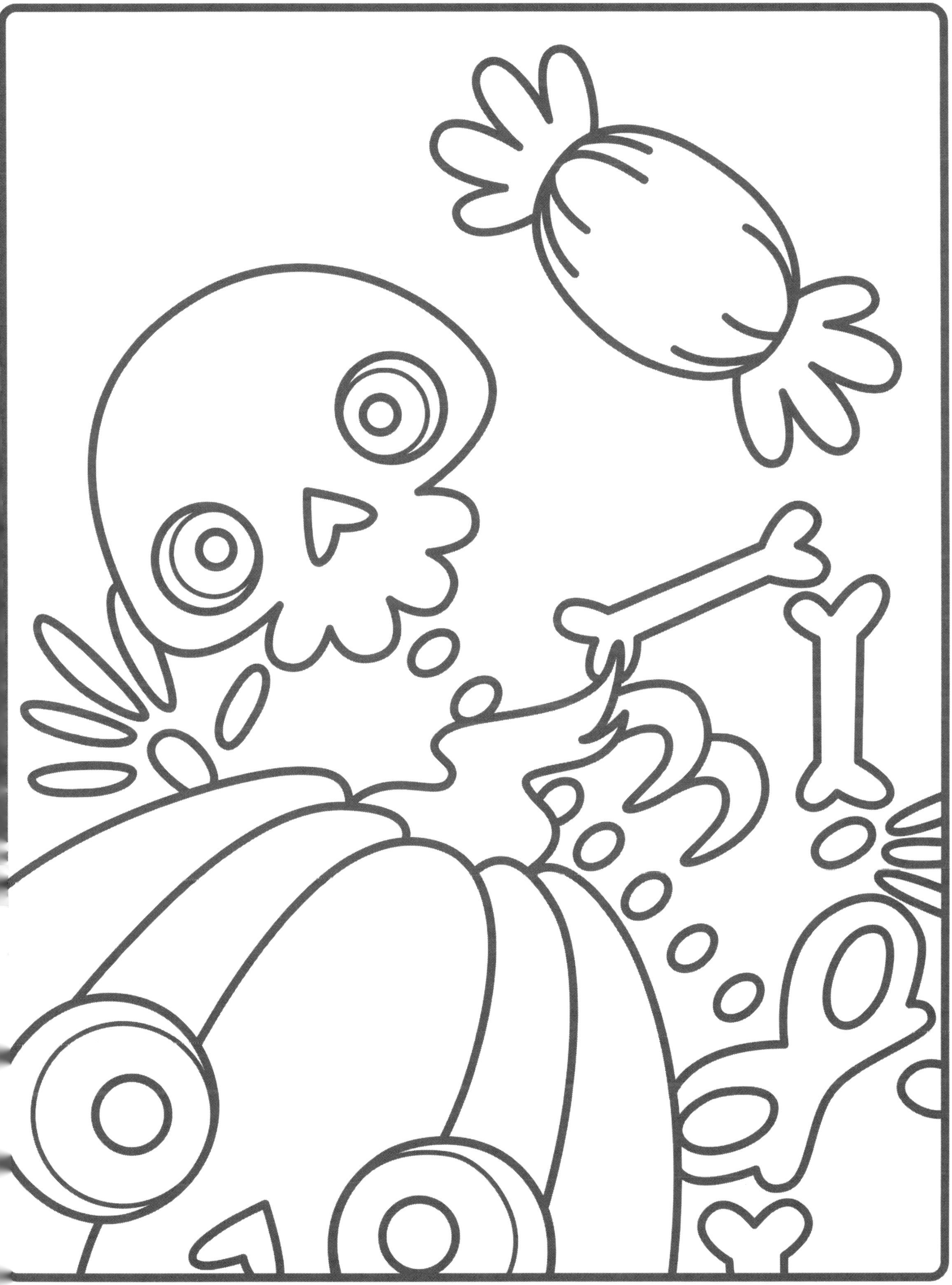

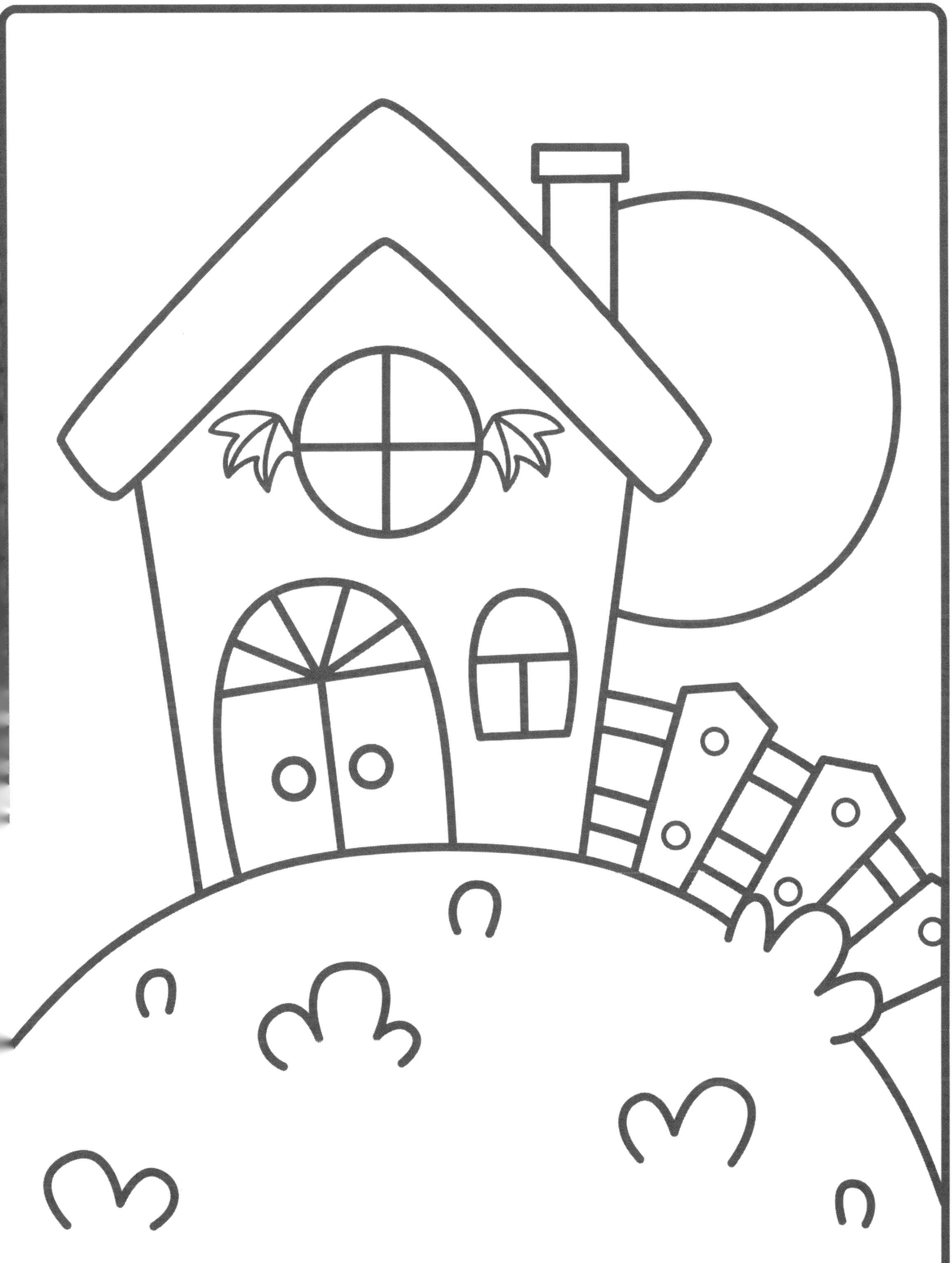

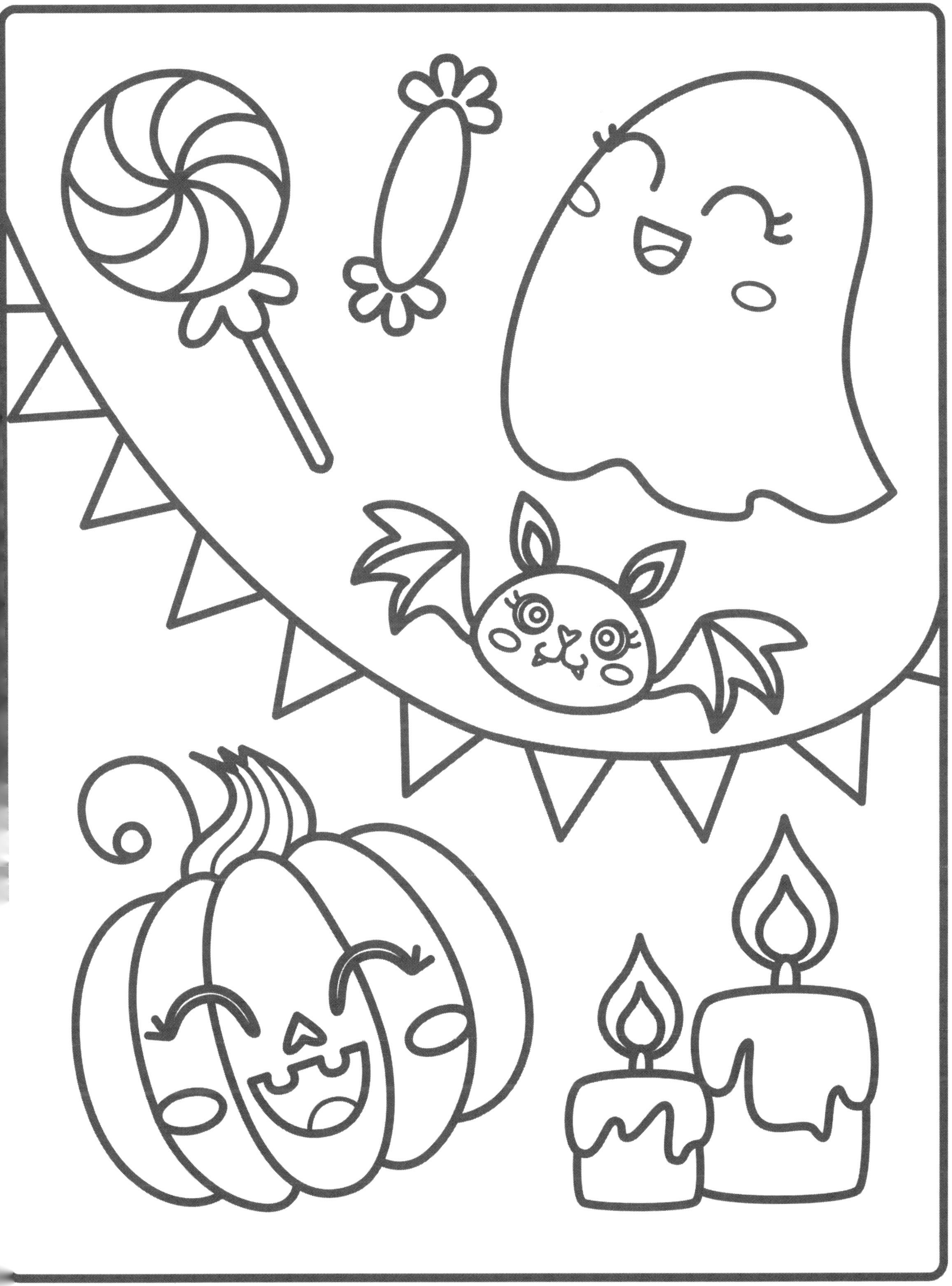

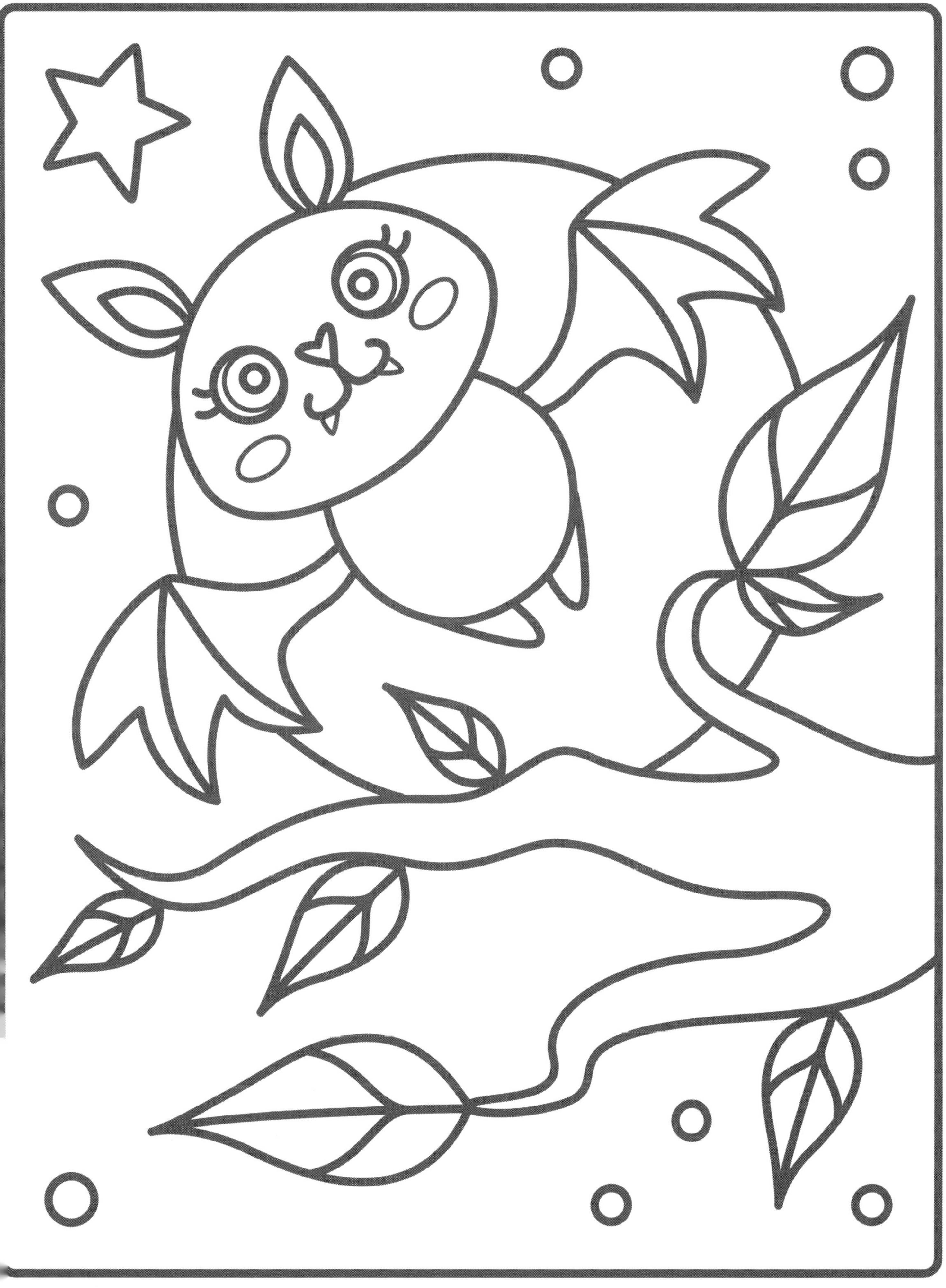

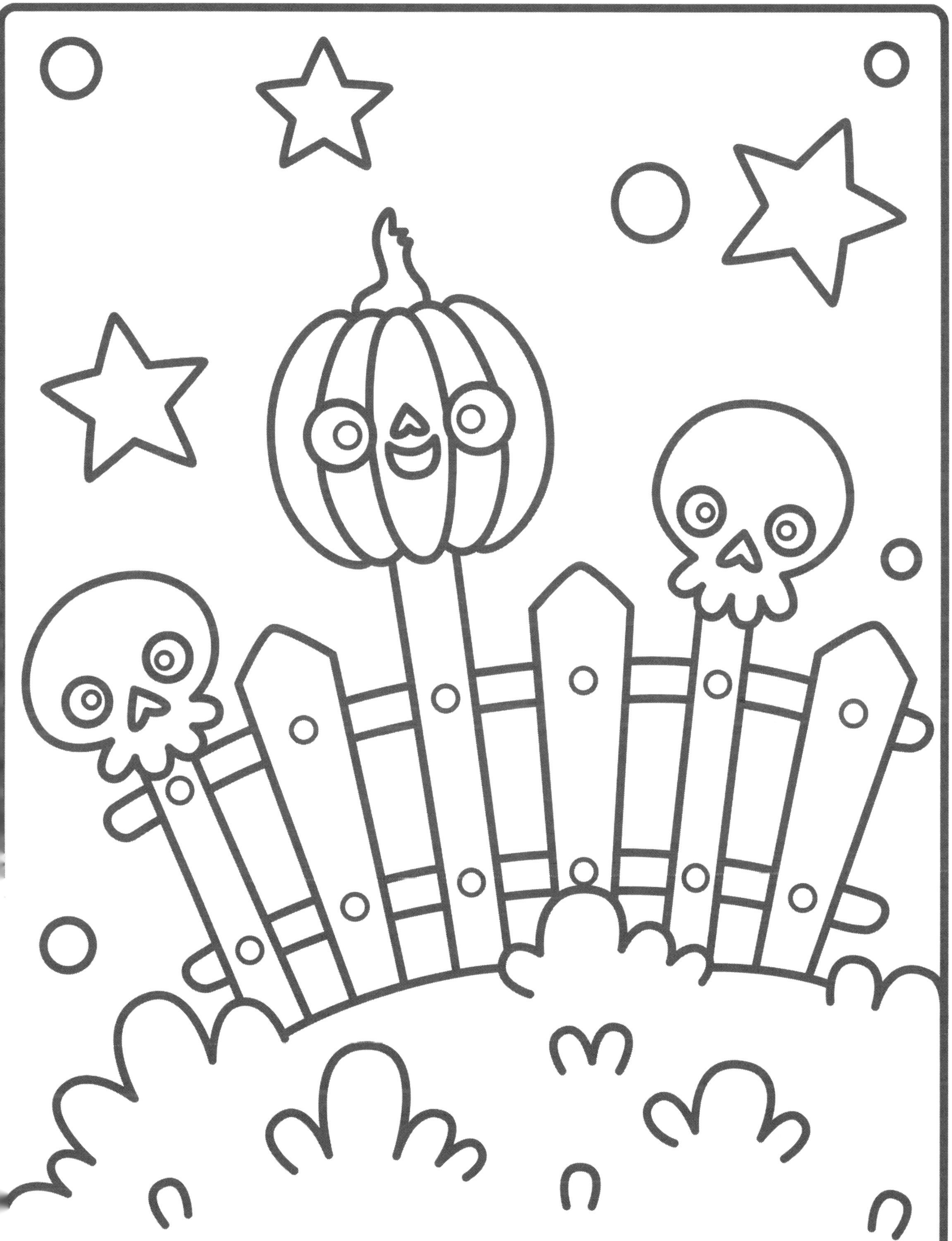

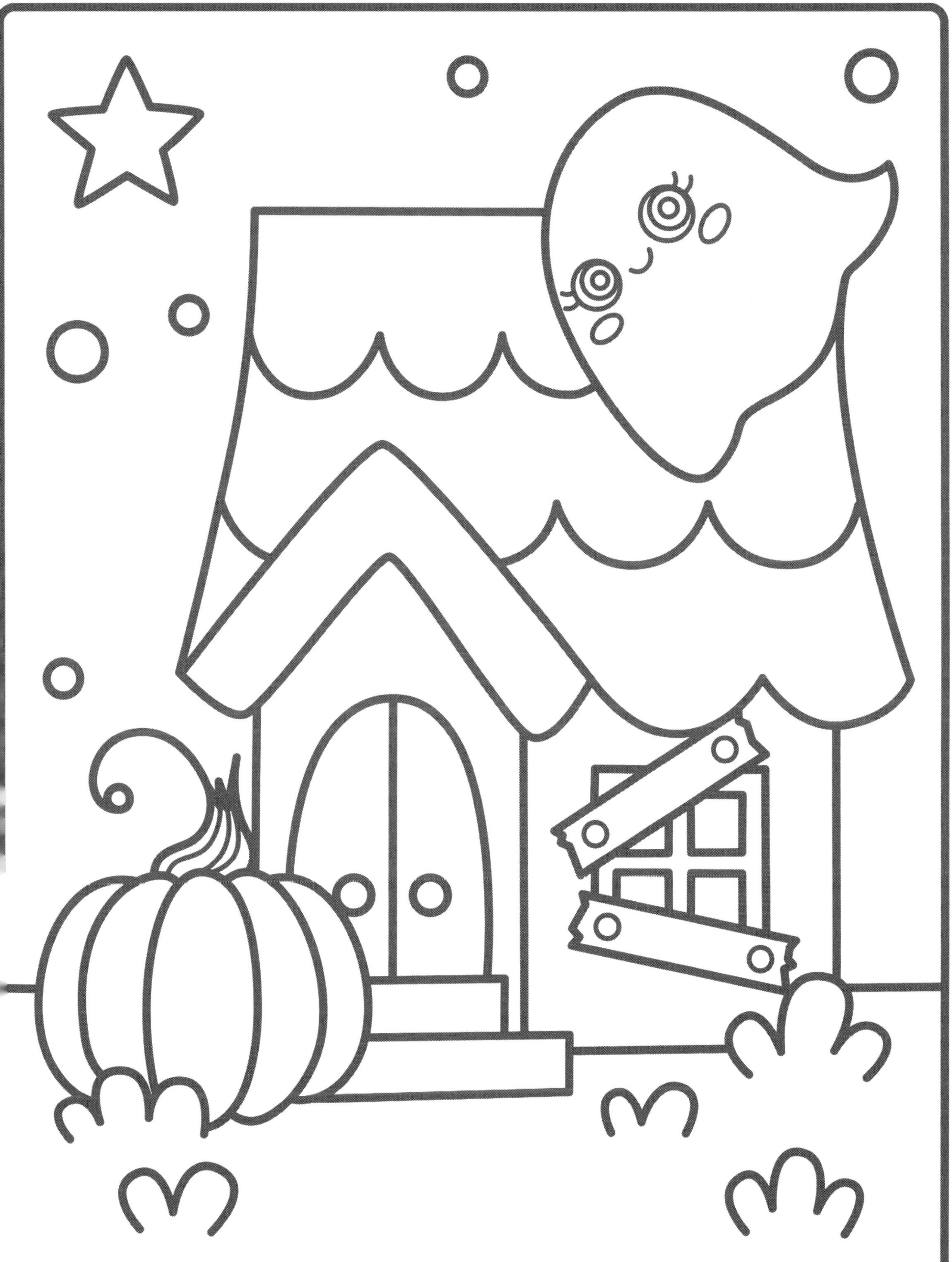

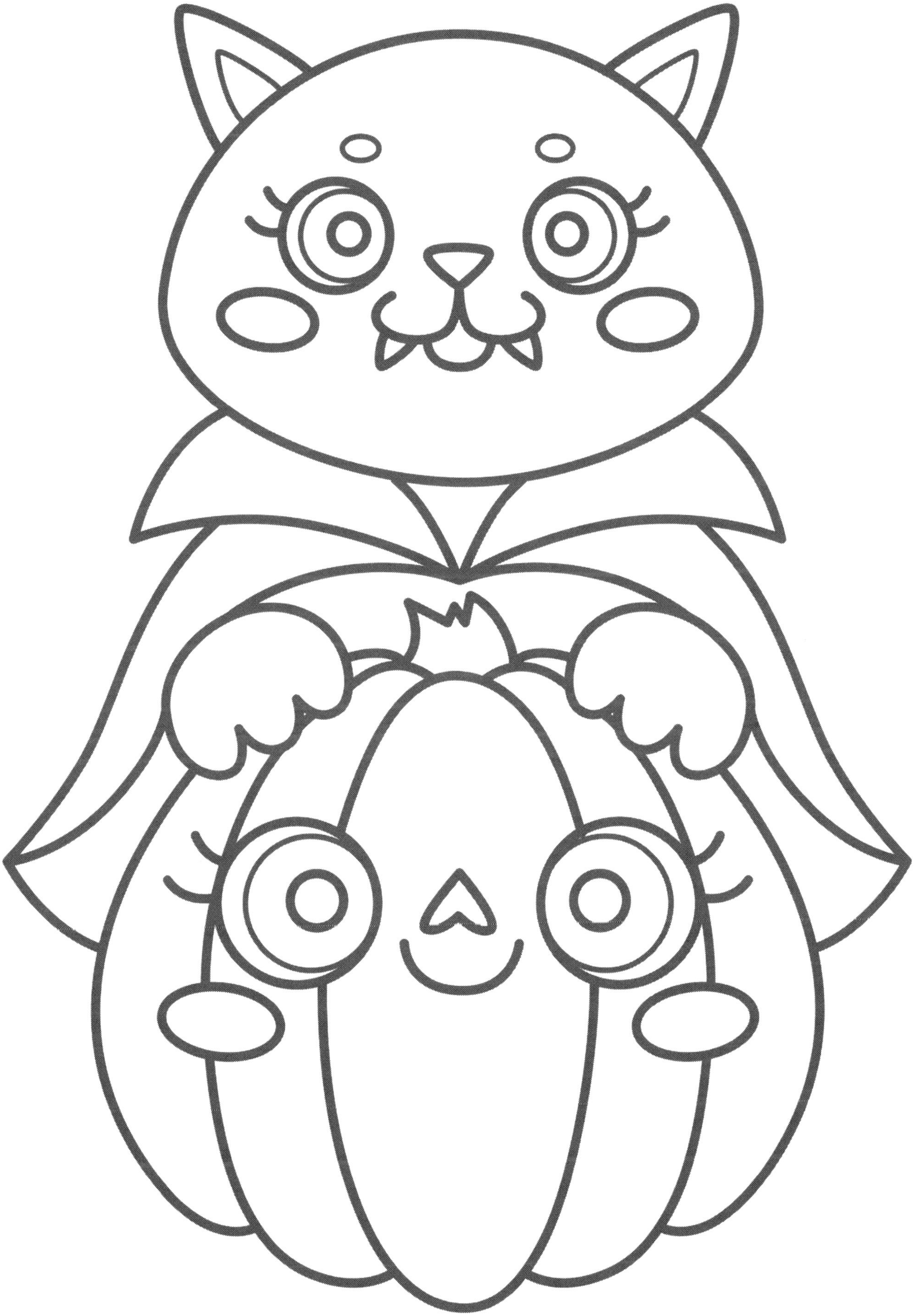

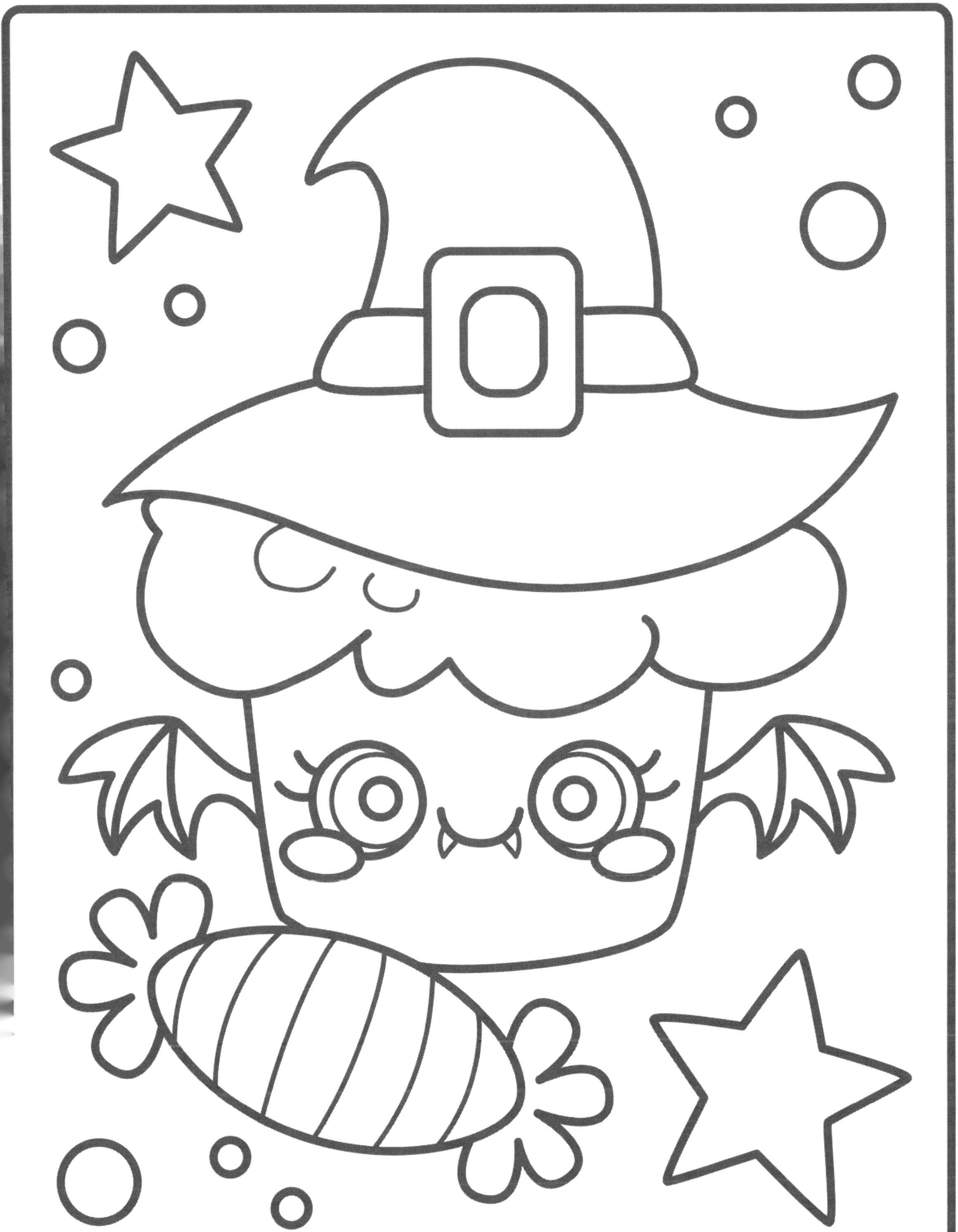

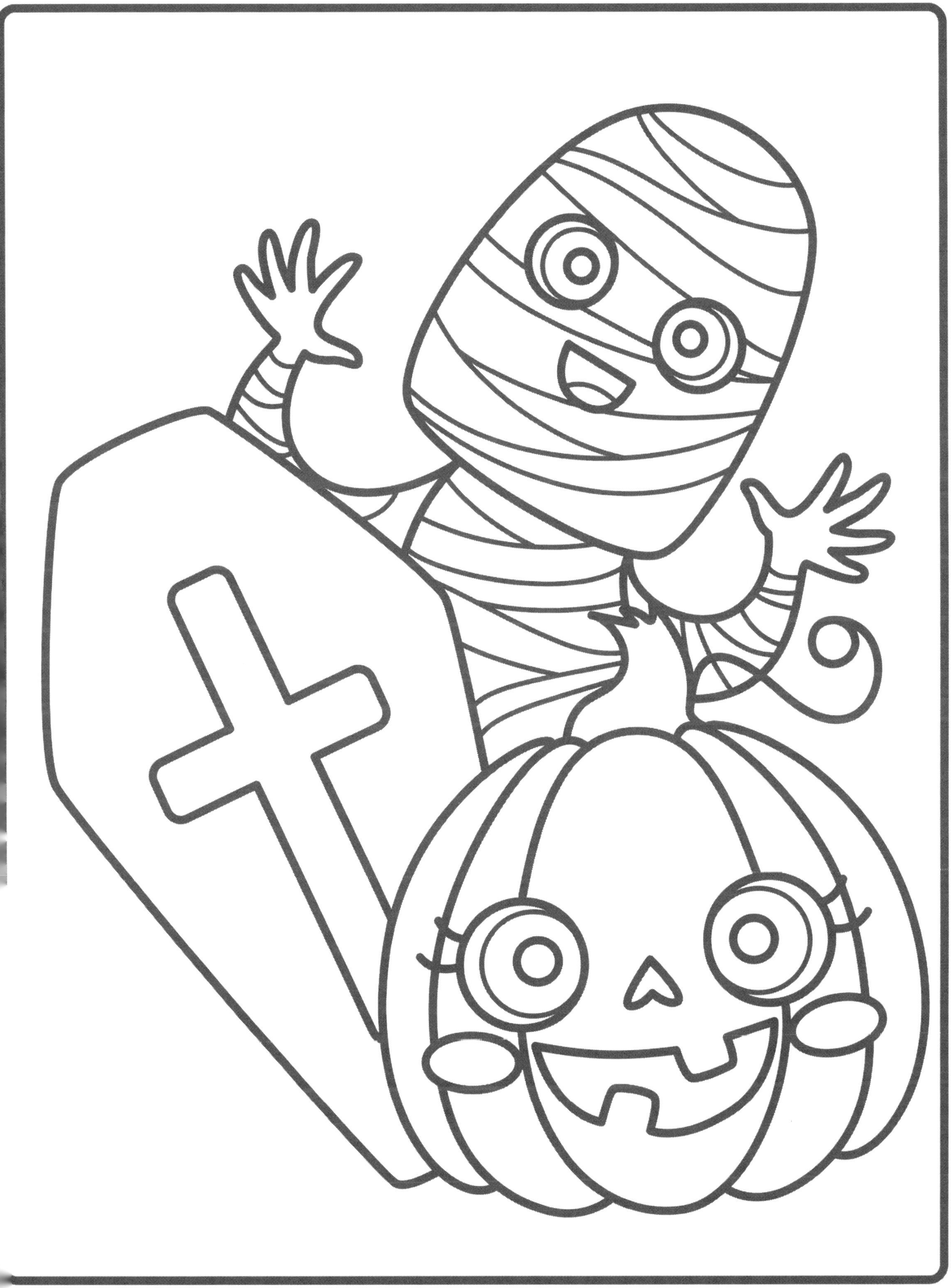

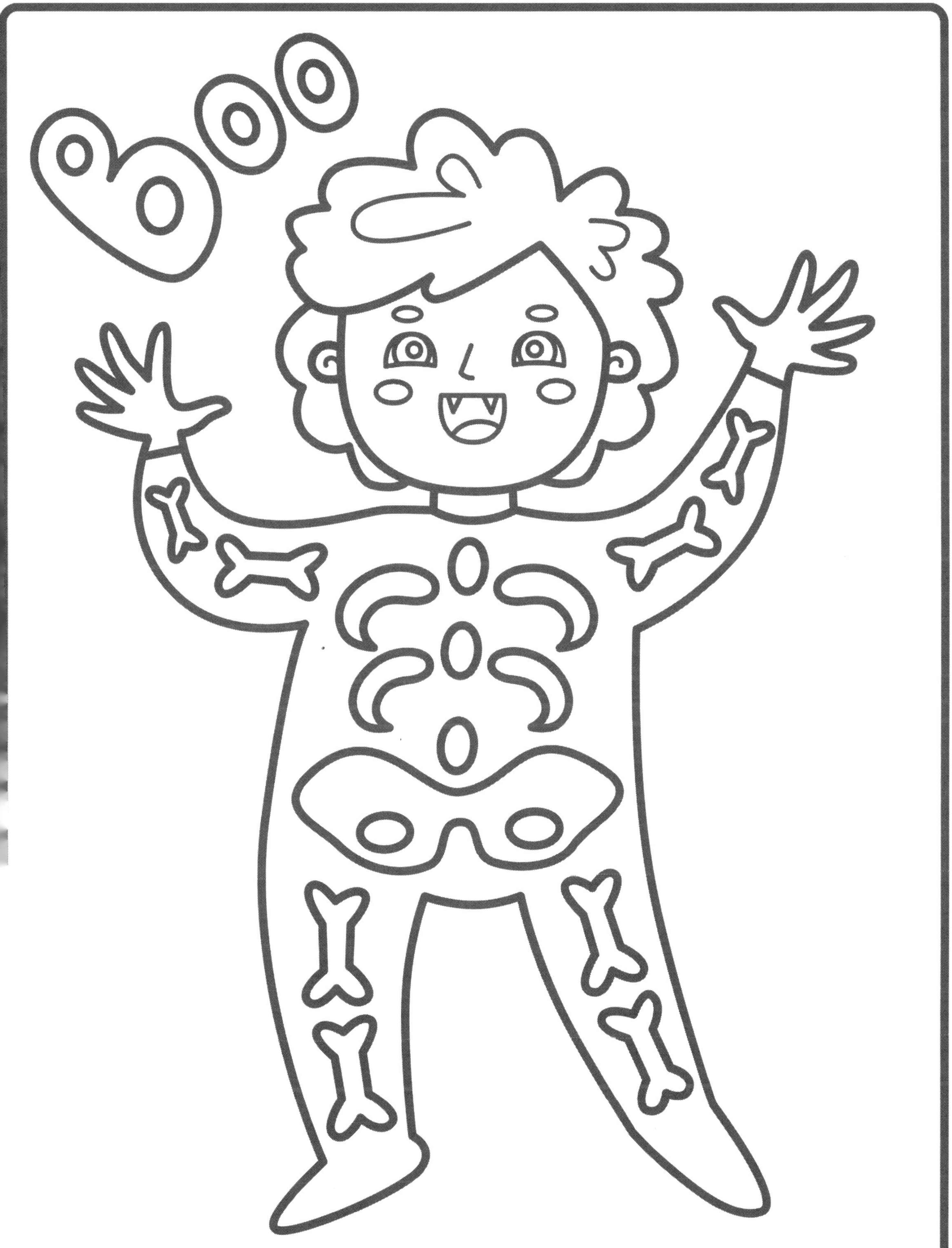
Booo

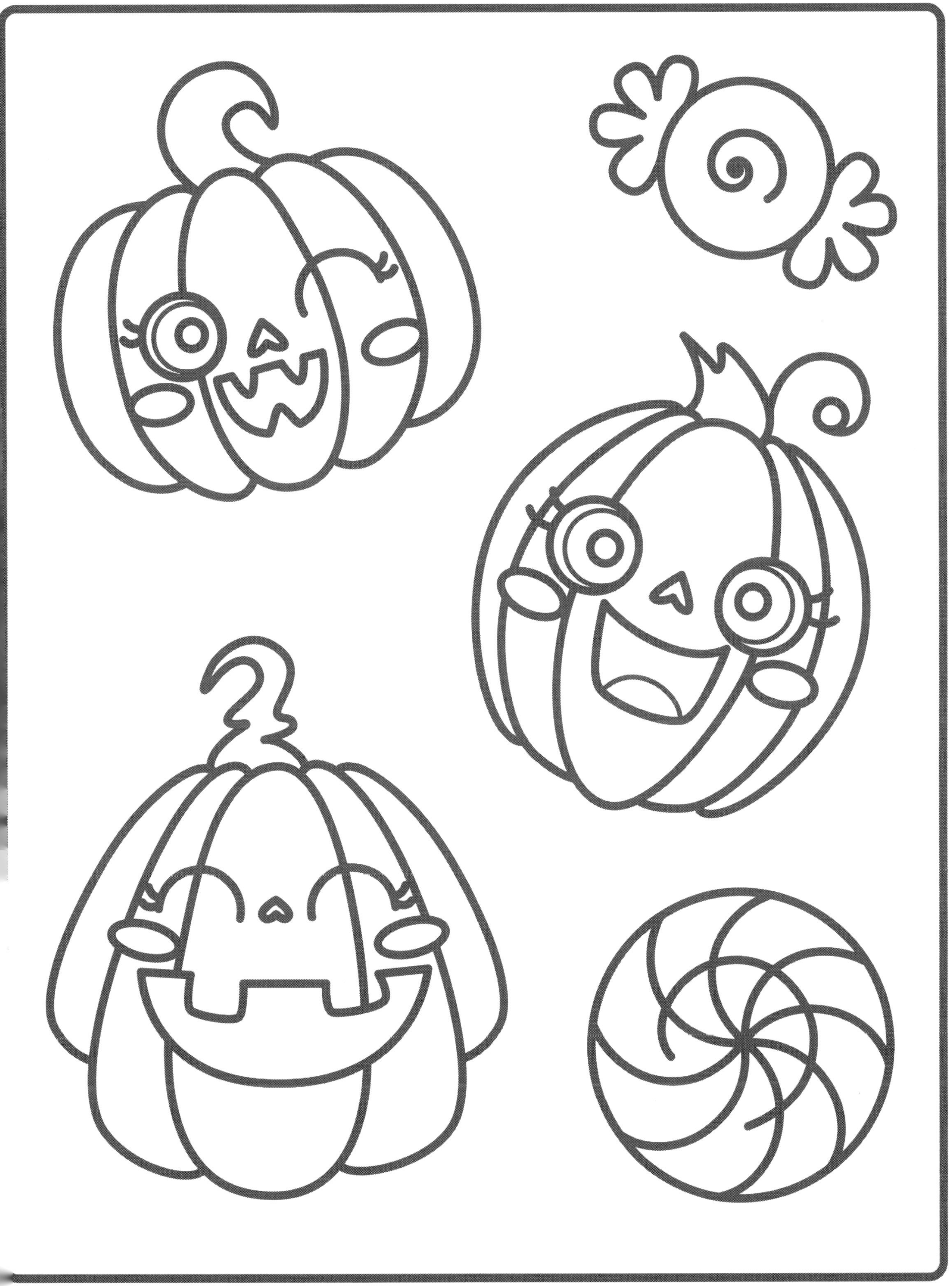

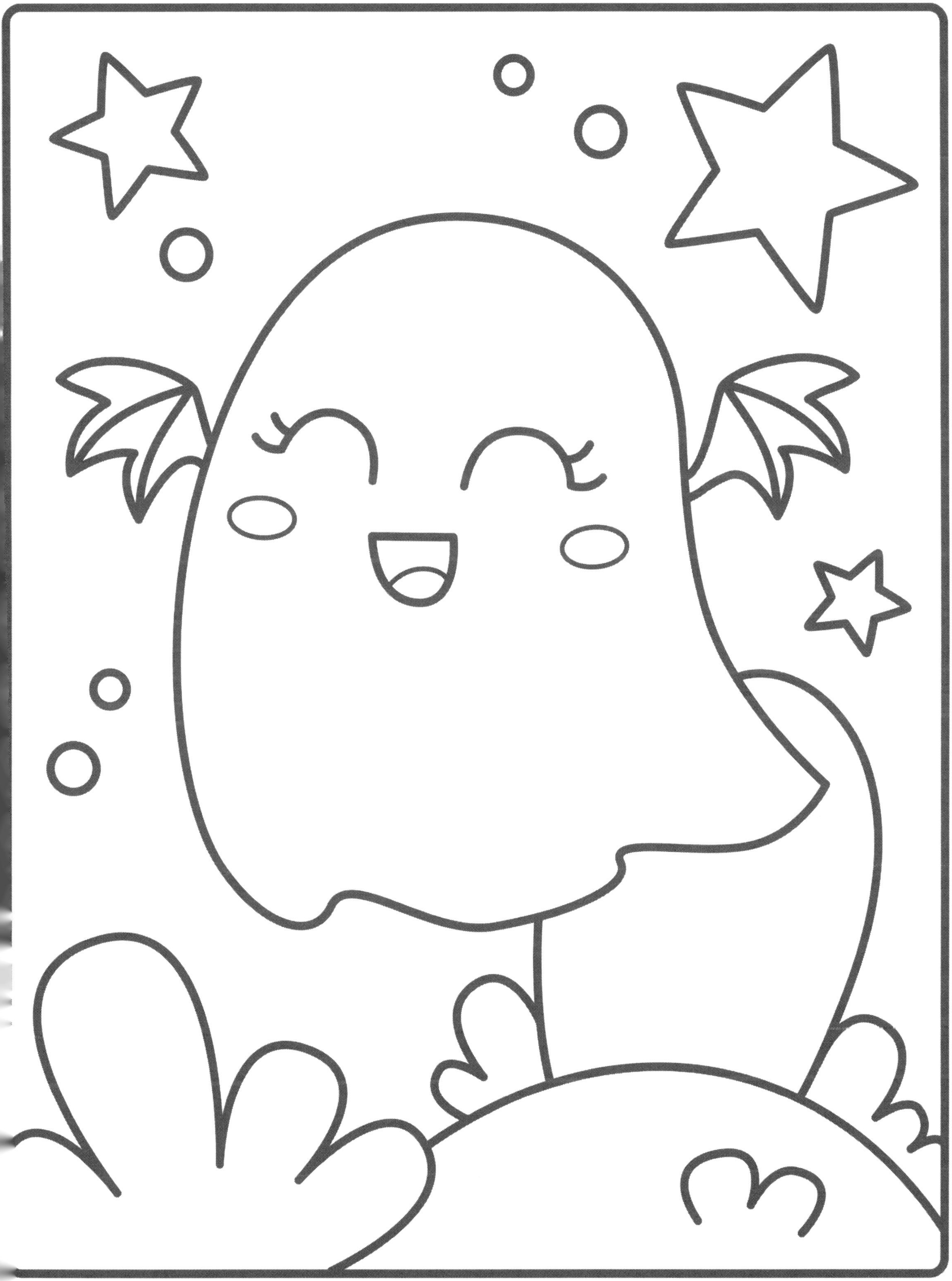

Made in United States
Troutdale, OR
09/28/2024

23207653R00035